STRIVERS ROW

During the 1920s and 1930s, around the time of the Harlem Renaissance, more than a quarter of a million African-Americans settled in Harlem, creating what was described at the time as "a cosmopolitan Negro capital which exert[ed] an influence over Negroes everywhere."

Nowhere was this more evident than on West 138th and 139th Streets between Adam Clayton Powell and Frederick Douglass Boulevards, two blocks that came to be known as Strivers Row. These blocks attracted many of Harlem's African-American doctors, lawyers, and entertainers, among them Eubie Blake, Noble Sissle, and W. C. Handy, who were themselves striving to achieve America's middle-class dream.

With its mission of publishing quality African-American literature, Strivers Row emulates those "strivers," capturing that same spirit of hope, creativity, and promise.

Rich Minds,
Rich Rewards

Rich Minds, Rich Rewards

52 Ways to Enhance, Enrich, and Empower Your Life

Valorie Burton

Villard / New York

All rights reserved under International and Pan-American Copyright Conventions. Published in the United States by Strivers Row, an imprint of Villard Books, a division of Random House, Inc., New York, and simultaneously in Canada by Random House of Canada Limited, Toronto.

VILLARD BOOKS is a registered trademark of Random House, Inc. STRIVERS ROW and colophon are trademarks of Random House, Inc.

An earlier edition of this work was self-published by the author in 1999.

LIBRARY OF CONGRESS CATALOGING-IN-PUBLICATION DATA

Burton, Valorie

Rich minds, rich rewards : 52 ways to enhance, enrich, and empower your life / Valorie Burton.

p.   cm.

ISBN 0-375-75710-4

1. Success. I. Title.

BJ1611 .B89 2001

158.1—dc21   2001017898

Villard Books website address: www.villard.com

Printed in the United States of America on acid-free paper

98765432

First Strivers Row Edition

BOOK DESIGN BY MERCEDES EVERETT

This book is dedicated to the memory of my
beloved grandparents. Thank you for continuing
to watch over me.

Johnny A. Burton, Sr.
1917–1982

Mary Arlean Burton
1919–1984

Pearl Greenlee Adger
1918–1992

Rev. W. W. Adger, Sr.
1913–1971

Acknowledgments

Johann Wolfgang von Goethe once said, "Whatever you think you can do or believe you can do, begin it. Action has magic, grace and power in it." Once I began on the journey of bringing this project to life, I was amazed at the people who were placed in my path to help the project along. Life is that way. Once you commit and give your all, opportunities seem to beat a path to your door. Indeed, none of us finds success all by ourselves. And so, I would like to acknowledge the people in my life who have made this experience rewarding, exciting, and tremendously blessed.

To my parents, Johnny A. Burton, Jr., and Leone Adger Murray. Thank you for giving me life, nurturing my talents, and believing in me.

To my editor, Melody Guy. It was serendipitous that we met, and I am so appreciative of you for bringing *Rich Minds, Rich Rewards* to the team at Villard. Your warmth, easygoing spirit, and enthusiasm have made this project a wonderful experience.

To Emma Rodgers of Black Images Book Bazaar. You are

"the woman"! I appreciate you and the doors of opportunity that you opened for me.

To David Hale Smith, my "favorite agent" from your favorite client. Thank you for your enthusiasm, guidance, and friendship.

Throughout my life, I have seen that God works through people. He has worked through these people in various ways to bless my writing and speaking career, promote my efforts, and bring this book to life: Margaret Adger Mack, my "Auntie"; Jacquline Anders, my friend; Michelle Martinez Metzger, my friend and managing partner of Burton-Metzger; Marla Roth and James and Betty Robison of *Life Today* with James Robison; Lynn Briggs, my friend and morning show host on KOAI—the Oasis; Til and Milton Pettis of Jokae's; Oscar Joyner, my friend and marketing director for the Tom Joyner Morning Show; and Jennifer Lawrence, my friend and PR assistant account executive at Burton-Metzger.

Sometimes others can see the vision for your life before you can see it yourself. I would like to thank these special people who by sharing their belief in me encouraged me to pursue my passion: Jacquline Anders, Stephen Andrews, Lynn Briggs, Sean Brown, Richie Butler, Chad Caldwell, Greg Campbell, Rev. Frederick D. Haynes, III, Wanda Lorenz, David Hale Smith and Ed Stewart.

To my brother Wade Murray, twenty years my junior, you make my heart smile and I love you so much! Thank you for spreading the word about me.

Thank you to the readers and audiences who have inspired me to continue inspiring them.

Most important, I thank God for inspiring me to write this book and for using me as a vessel to deliver this message.

Acknowledgments

Contents

Acknowledgments	ix
Introduction	xv
Count Your Blessings	3
Recognize That Everything in Life Is a Choice	6
Speak in a Way That Lifts You Up	9
Change Your Ways to Change Your Life	11
Meditate	13
Listen to Your Inner Voice	17
Allow Peace to Guide Your Decisions	20
Have a Mission	24
Create Your Mission Statement	27
Have a Vision	32
Create a Vision Statement	34
Write Down Your Goals	37
Don't Downsize Your Dream	41
Take the First Step	43
Feel the Fear and Don't Let It Stop You!	45
Let Go and Let God	48
Use Failure as a Learning Tool	51
Do What You Love and the Rewards Will Come	55
To Do Your Best Work, Be Your Best Self	59
Personal PR	62
Save the Drama	66
Say Please and Thank You	69

Express Love   73

Mind Your Own Business   75

Emulate Successful People   77

Surround Yourself with People Who Are Going Places   80

Don't Make Excuses   83

Don't Play the Blame Game   86

Focus on the Most Important Task First   88

Don't Try to Do Everything Yourself   91

Get a Mentor   94

Practice How You Want to Be   99

Take Control of Your Financial Life   102

Don't Let Age Block Your Path to Success   106

Live in the Moment   110

Cure Yourself of the Overdrive Syndrome   113

Understand That Education = Preparation   117

Love Yourself First   120

Practice Patience   122

Do Nice Things (But Keep Them to Yourself!)   125

Volunteer   128

Understand Rather than Judge   131

Forgive and Let Go of Grudges   134

Visit a New Place at Least Once a Year   137

Reward Yourself!   139

Pamper-ize Yourself   142

Make Your Home Your Sanctuary   145

Learn to Network   148

Write Handwritten Letters and Make an Impact   152

Spend Time with Yourself   156

Stress: Less, Not More   158

Create Your Own Opportunities   161

Planning a Discussion   164

Suggested Reading   168

A Conversation with Author Valorie Burton   170

Contents

Introduction

The idea for this book came to me in what I will call a "revelation." It was late in the afternoon on Saturday, July 10, 1999, and I was in Seattle for a journalism convention. I was browsing through books at the Barnes & Noble in downtown Seattle. Up until that moment, I was unsure of my life's purpose. Though I have always felt richly blessed and have enjoyed owning a public relations agency, I always felt that my purpose in life did not center around the business. The purpose did not hit me until that day, when, as I stood in front of the women's books section, an overpowering sensation came over me. In an instant, I felt the presence of God. The feeling was somewhat indescribable and I can say for certain that I had never felt that way before—as if God's arms were wrapped around me and I might just float away. I stood still and listened—not with my ears, but with my heart and soul. I learned my life's purpose that day.

God said, "Your purpose is to inspire people to live fulfilling lives. You will do this through writing and speaking." I remained still, enjoying this intensely personal and pivotal moment in a very public place. I stood there awestruck and excited all at once.

I continued to browse and then walked back to my hotel a couple of blocks away. I began to conceptualize this book. When I returned to Dallas, I began writing with purpose. In four months, I wrote and self-published *Rich Minds, Rich Rewards*. The following summer, Villard Books, a division of Random House, approached me about publishing it. This book is the result.

So just what is *Rich Minds, Rich Rewards* all about? This book will help you experience the rich rewards that life has to offer when your mind is elevated and focused on those aspects of life that truly matter. The term "rich rewards" does not refer simply to financial wealth. Rich rewards refers to the benefits of living the life you really want to live—a life of fulfillment, joy, love, and spiritual well-being.

When you have a "rich mind," you discover your mission in life and live it on a daily basis. You enjoy what life has to offer. You don't stress over the little stuff in life that, in the grand scheme of things, really doesn't matter much.

A rich mind rises above pettiness, grudges, envy, bickering, and selfishness to strive for patience, purpose, vision, kindness, love, and fulfillment. A rich mind appreciates blessings and knows that there are more blessings pouring down from Heaven than could ever be counted.

Rich Minds, Rich Rewards is written from a very personal viewpoint. As an entrepreneur, speaker, and writer who has lived in many places (Florida, Germany, Colorado, South Carolina, California, and Texas), my experience is diverse. Through my successes and failures, I have learned that the mind is your most powerful asset for achieving any dream that you have for yourself. A rich mind—nourished with positive thoughts, learning, and encouragement—can indeed reap rich rewards.

In each of the following fifty-two mini-chapters you will find simple but powerful ways to enhance your everyday life and start doing those things that will bring you the rewards you so richly deserve.

Rich Minds, Rich Rewards

Count Your Blessings

66 "The difference between 'not enough' and 'more than enough' is your attitude," noted Bishop T. D. Jakes at a conference I attended in July 1999. As we live our lives from day to day, it can be easy to take so much of what we have for granted. For example, when we are unhappy in a job and we are looking for a new one, sometimes the last thing that we think to do is to thank God for the job that we dislike. When we want to purchase a new home, it is too rare that we stop to appreciate the roof we currently have over our heads. When we are working out to get a "new body," we should not fail to be thankful that the one we have right now allows us to walk, talk, and breathe. We can get so wrapped up in trying to get what we don't have that we don't take time to appreciate what we *do* have.

I know these things may sound very basic, but it is the most "basic" aspects of our lives, those things that we often don't even give a second thought to, that we should be most grateful for. It is these "basic" things—people, places, our well-being—that it would be most devastating for us to have to live without. When you come to understand what is most important to you, and make it a priority in your life to honor and take care of those aspects of your life, then you find your center. Your center is that place you discover when your life is healthy and balanced. It takes some true soul-searching to find it, and it takes practice to maintain it. But once you find that peaceful, joyful place called your center, you'll always feel off balance when you leave it.

One way to stay centered is to count your blessings every day. Why every day? Because it can be too easy to fall into the habit of taking life for granted and feeling sorry for yourself when things don't go the way you had hoped. By counting your blessings, you remember just how rich you are—in spirit, family, friendships, health, career, education, personality, and the list goes on.

Count your blessings in the mornings. It is a very uplifting way to begin the day. After all, a new day is one more blessing for which you have to be thankful.

Try this exercise: Turn off all the noise around you and go to a place where you can find as much solitude as possible. Close your eyes. Breathe deeply and slowly. Now think about all that you have to be thankful for. Stay in this quiet state for at least five minutes. When you finish, write down everything that came to mind.

My Blessings:

1. _____
2. _____
3. _____
4. _____
5. _____
6. _____
7. _____
8. _____
9. _____
10. _____

It's a pretty good list, isn't it? When you find yourself feeling down or sorry for yourself, take out your list. Read it and be thankful for what you *do* have instead of focusing on what you *don't* have.

Recognize That Everything in Life Is a Choice

Have you ever considered the fact that every single thing we do in life is a choice? From getting out of bed in the morning to bringing children into the world, everything in your life is about the choices you make as you live it. Simply doing nothing is even a choice. Some of the most important choices we can make in life deal with how we choose to respond to the adversities we face. When something bad happens to you, you can't change what happened, but you have complete control over your response to the situation. Will you choose to be a "victim"? Will you retaliate? Will you hold a grudge against those who are responsible? In short, will you use your precious time and energy on prolonged negativity or will you address the problem, do what needs to be done to alleviate it and then move on with your life? I hope you will do the latter.

Valorie Burton

If you find yourself in a bad relationship, romantic or otherwise, remaining in that relationship is your choice. It's your choice to enter and maintain positive relationships. If you hate your job, it's your choice whether you leave that job or you choose to stay. If you have a dream, you can choose to pursue it or you can choose to let it lie dormant, collecting dust until eventually it is so buried in dust that you completely lose sight of it. It's your choice.

You can choose to go back to school and get that degree, or to go to graduate school like you always said you would so that you can increase your earning potential. Or you can choose to stay right where you are and keep talking about it. The point is, you have to free yourself from the mindset that your life is controlled by your current circumstances. You have the power to create the life you really want. The power is in the choices that you make. Use that power today and choose to live the life you so richly deserve.

Choose to be successful. Choose to be kind. Choose to be forgiving. Choose to have integrity. Choose to love unconditionally. Choose to pursue the career of your dreams. Choose to love yourself first. Choose to relax. Choose to be pampered. Choose to be attractive, both inside and out. Choose to abandon mediocrity in your life and replace it with a pursuit of excellence.

Ask yourself what new choices you need to begin to make, starting today. What one choice could you make, whether large or small, that would improve your life in some way?

Simply recognizing the tremendous power in choice will make you feel more powerful. When you feel powerful, you have the courage to do things that fear normally would keep you from doing. Remember, whatever it is that you want to achieve, you can do it! The choice is yours.

Valorie Burton

Speak in a Way That Lifts You Up

It is amazing how often we describe our circumstances or feelings with language that is negatively exaggerated and just plain untrue. "This job is killing me." "If s/he leaves me, my life will be over." "I could never accomplish that." "I'll just die if that happens."

You may think of these statements as nothing more than harmless remarks. In reality, this kind of negative talk does nothing positive for you. Subconsciously, negative banter encourages you to believe that things are much worse than they actually are. By making a conscious effort to speak positively about yourself and your circumstances, you actually lift your spirits and elevate your thinking. I find it sad when I ask someone how they are doing and all they can manage to respond with is a whiney "Oh, I'm makin' it" or "Well, I'm gettin' by." What?! There are thousands of people who are sick, bedridden, or truly struggling in some way and they managed to wake up this morning praising God for simply letting them spend another day with their loved ones. They know joy purely from the gift of life. Meanwhile, people with seemingly so much more to be thankful for manage to shuffle through life dwelling on what they don't have and verbalizing their "feel-sorry-for-me" attitude with negative statements that bring themselves down, and sometimes those around them, too. Speaking positively is a habit that must come from within. Of course, if you remember to count your blessings, the idea of talking down instead of talking up should be the furthest thing from your mind!

Valorie Burton

Change Your
Ways to Change Your Life

We've all heard the saying "If you keep doing what you're doing, you'll keep getting what you're getting." Consider this scenario:

Angie is an attractive woman. She is a real estate agent, doing very well selling homes in upper-middle-class neighborhoods. She's smart and outgoing. She's unhappy, however, with her weight. A while back, she said she wanted to lose weight. She had a plan. She was going to go on a diet (which she had done on at least ten previous occasions). She went on the diet for a few weeks and lost some of the weight. Within two months, however, she had gained all of it back (plus a few extra pounds). She hasn't gone on another diet since. She continues to eat lots of junk food, won't exercise, and makes little effort to limit her fat intake. Amazingly, she still complains about her weight and expresses bewilderment at not being able to get the weight off. Sounds ridiculous, right?

Well, many of us suffer from this same predicament in other ways. We expect our lives to change for the better, but we don't do anything differently. How can you expect to change your life if you don't change your ways? You have to try a new way of doing things. Success requires an element of risk. You won't rise to new heights by staying in your comfort zone. You've got to be willing to get out of your element and try something different so that you can reach goals you've never reached before.

Do you ever find yourself saying things like "That's just the way I am" or "I've always done it that way"? From now on, become aware of saying such things. Subconsciously you're telling yourself that you *can't* do it any differently. That simply is not true. If you are going to create a life of success and fulfillment, you have to be willing to do things differently. Find out what it is that you need to do to get the results that you are looking for. Then take a leap of faith, and if you feel a little uncomfortable, that's okay. It probably means that you are on the right track.

Meditate

Think of meditation as "down time," a sort of vacation for your mind. With the stress many of us experience, even for those of us who try our best to avoid it, the mind is in a constant state of work. Think about it. Aren't you always thinking? Sometimes we have ten things going on at once and our minds shift into overdrive. From career to family to household work, our minds rarely get a break while we are awake. And for many, especially those who are overstressed, the mind keeps going when they lie down at night, too. Your mind needs a break, and not just once or twice a year when you go on vacation.

You deserve some peaceful, reflective, quiet time every day. Make a commitment to yourself. It can be only a few minutes, but make sure that you set aside some time. Five minutes of meditation is a small amount of time, but it can reap for you the priceless reward of peace of mind. You may feel more comfortable if you start by meditating once or twice per week and build up to every day. As you become more comfortable with meditation and it becomes a part of your daily routine, you will find that your days are more productive and your mind is more focused than ever before. Meditation allows us to get more in tune with ourselves. As we block out distractions, we are able to give full attention to our inner voice.

Meditation has helped me to better understand the desires of my heart. As my mind clears, I am better able to hear my inner voice. This is a key element of self-discovery and fulfillment. We often determine what we think we want for ourselves by what the world tells us we should want. But what the world says may not be what makes us happy.

To begin incorporating meditation into your life, first find a place where you will be comfortable. I suggest sitting on the floor, so you may want to use a pillow to make yourself comfortable. Sit in a position that feels good to you. Use good posture. Sitting up straight with your chin slightly lifted will give you positive body language, which in turn helps lift your spirits. Stock up on aromatherapy candles in your favorite scents. My favorites are lavender and French vanilla, but I experiment with many different varieties. As the scents fill the room while you are meditating, your spirits will be lifted and your body will become more relaxed.

Valorie Burton

The most important aspect of meditation is deep breathing. Because our breathing is automatic, we seldom think about deliberately controlling it. Deliberate deep breaths are both healthy and relaxing. Most of us, even when we breathe deeply, don't breathe correctly because we take breaths from the chest rather than the stomach. You can actually see the chest inflate and deflate when you breathe incorrectly. When you take a conscious deep breath, you should breathe deeply from your stomach. You will see your stomach inflate as you breathe in and deflate as you breathe out. Inhale through your nose and exhale through your nose or mouth. Repeat your deep breaths five to ten times, concentrating completely on each breath as you sit comfortably on the floor. Each time you feel distracted by thoughts of work or chores or anything else, focus more intently on your breathing.

The goal of meditation is to relax your mind, thereby releasing energy and creativity that can be hindered by stress and tension. Through meditation I was able to clearly recognize and accept my true self. Not only was my inner voice able to speak, but also I was able to eliminate outside noise and actually listen to what it was trying to tell me. Through meditation I was able to uncover the truth about what brings me joy and I was able to pinpoint my God-given gifts—mainly the gifts of communication, compassion, and the ability to motivate others. Once my gifts became clear to me,

I prayed about how I could use them in a way that would bring me joy, passion, and income and at the same time benefit others. As I meditated, I listened for the answer. It did not come right away and it did not come all at once. But it did come and it was clear. In addition to managing The Burton Agency, at this time in my life my gifts are best used as a speaker and writer, inspiring others to lead fulfilled lives. And I came to this discovery through the power of meditation.

For me, meditation is most effective in the morning, before I start my day. After I meditate, I look at my day planner and organize my priorities for the day. I feel refreshed and focused for the projects ahead. My days have a better sense of direction when I don't jump out of bed and hit the ground running. Instead, I pause for a moment, reflect, and get energized. Commit to trying meditation at least twice a week. I promise, the benefits will delight you.

Valorie Burton

Listen to Your Inner Voice

Why is it that we often ignore our instincts, only to kick ourselves later for not following them? I think it is because we don't trust ourselves enough. We don't trust our "inner voice." Another reason that we ignore our instincts is that to follow our instincts is to defy logic. After all, it is very difficult to explain this "sixth sense." Facts, we understand. Instincts, we question. Because we can't explain them, we often do not trust them. I believe that our inner voice, or "instinct"—that voice that tells us when to do something, how to do it, or for whom to do it—usually comes from God. When we don't understand the *why,* that's God talking to us.

Hebrews 4:7 says, "Harden not your heart the day you hear God's voice." Sometimes our instincts keep us out of harm's way. Sometimes our instincts lead us into a situation where we end up meeting people who, in one way or another, help us meet our goals. Trust your instincts, because in doing so, you begin to trust yourself and God.

In the summer of 1996, I followed my instincts on a seemingly small idea and it led to a wonderful opportunity. I was an avid reader of the *Dallas Business Journal* and was annoyed by two stories that ran in back-to-back issues of the newspaper. The stories were about my people my age, and in my opinion they did not reflect well on us as workers. The articles explained how we had to be managed differently, that we're not as loyal, and that some of us were slackers. Although some of the points in the articles were valid, I felt an urge to write a letter to the editor in defense of my generation. The urge hit me while I was standing in front of the bathroom mirror and putting on my makeup one morning, as I prepared to go to work. At first I thought, "Oh, I'll write something quickly when I get to work." But my inner voice told me to stop what I was doing and write the letter to the editor right then. So I did. The words came to me so fast that I didn't bother to wait for my computer to boot up. I simply grabbed a pen and a piece of paper and began to write. When the letter was finished, I typed it up and printed it out. When I got to work, I faxed it to the newspaper. My letter ran in that week's issue of the *Dallas Business Journal*.

A couple of days later, the editor called and asked me to lunch. The letter had caused a stir in the newsroom. At lunch, he asked if I would be willing to write a regular column about

Valorie Burton

issues facing people in their twenties and early thirties in the workplace. "Sure, I'd love to," I told him. That was six months before I started The Burton Agency. The column in the *Dallas Business Journal* led the publisher of another publication to ask me to write a public relations column for that journal, which has national and regional editions. Those columns have led to new business for my company and added credibility for me among clients and prospective clients. And to think, all of the events were put into motion because I followed my instincts one morning while I was getting ready for work. Instead of ignoring my inner voice, I listened, stopped what I was doing, and wrote that letter to the editor.

Allow Peace to Guide Your Decisions

Rich minds make decisions that are guided by love, peace, and clarity. As a result, decisions are made from a position of authentic strength. Poor minds make decisions out of fear, doubt, and confusion—a position of weakness. How can you use this truth to ensure that you make the best choices for you?

First, you must be in tune with your inner voice—the Divine wisdom that speaks to you when you are open to listening. When we are in touch with who we are, what we stand for, and what we really want in life, then we are best able to make life-impacting decisions. When a decision is right, we experience a sense of peace about it. The right decision does not leave you with a sense of turmoil, doubt, and uneasiness. This does not necessarily mean that the decision is easy, but it means that you made the decision for the right reason and with pure intentions. The end result is what I call a "pure decision." A pure decision is one that is rooted in Divine wisdom. Pure decisions require faith—faith that if you trust your inner voice, things will work out as they should. By making pure decisions, you exercise your faith and learn to trust yourself. Because pure decisions are based on faith—the substance of things hoped for and the evidence of things not seen—it takes courage to make them.

Imagine that every decision you make is a glass of crystal-clear springwater. As you consider each factor that guides you to your decision, you must add the factor to your pure glass of water. Those based in love, peace, and clarity are pure ice cubes that make your glass of water cooler and more refreshing. The factors based in fear, doubt, and confusion are like dirty little pebbles that you must add to your pure glass of water. If you allow even one dirty pebble into the glass, no matter how many fresh ice cubes made the water cool, it's now clouded by the dirt from the pebble.

If you make a pure decision by allowing peace to guide you, you will still feel good about the decision after you've made it. Have you ever made a decision and felt internal conflict about it afterward? The internal conflict was your inner voice communicating to you that your decision was not on target. Decisions made out of fear, doubt, and confusion are not always obvious because they can appear to be very good decisions.

For example, you may choose to pursue a career in a

prestigious field. You work hard and find success. Your family and friends are proud of you. But after a while you begin to feel empty. Perhaps your decision to enter the field you chose was influenced by your need for approval and validation rather than your passion for the work. The need for approval and validation is the dirty pebble in your glass of pure springwater.

So often the factors that guide our decisions are 90 percent pure, but there are one or two little dirty pebbles that cloud them. The dirty pebbles are fear—fear of not being accepted, of not having enough or being enough, or of not succeeding. Your inner voice will always let you know, but you must be willing to listen. If you don't feel a sense of peace, it's time to look inward to determine what fear-based factors are clouding your decision and causing peace to elude you.

If you are not conscious of your decision-making patterns, you can spend a lifetime making decisions based on what the world dictates rather than what your inner voice tells you is right for you. To determine whether you are making fear-based decisions in major areas of your life, you must be willing to ask yourself some telling questions:

- Why am I in the career I'm in right now? Is it because it is my calling and it's what I want to be doing at this time in my life? Or is it because I fear that I am not able to make the living I want doing what I love?

- Am I in my current love relationship because of love and fate or would I rather be with someone else but don't want to leave the relationship I have because it's secure or I fear being alone?

- Do I spend my money based on what I want and can afford or based on the validation I get from driving a certain car, wearing certain clothes, or living in a certain neighborhood?

We often mask our fear-based decisions with logical reasoning. It keeps us from facing the truth about why we do what we do. But uncovering the truth about your decisions is the first step to learning to allow peace to guide them.

Have a Mission

What comes to mind when you hear the words "mission statement"? You probably think of a descriptive statement that companies use to communicate their purpose for being in business. Often, a mission statement ends up being a long-winded, abstract essay that the company spends hours preparing and then files away, rarely to be seen again. If taken seriously and written well, however, a mission statement can give purpose and meaning to everything that a company does. A personal mission statement does the same thing on an individual level.

When you create your mission statement, you create a gauge by which you can assess everything that you choose to do in your life. It is a single sentence that is broad enough to encompass your work and personal life, and narrow enough to define the underlying purpose in all that you do. When you are interviewing for a new job, your stated mission will help you determine whether or not a particular company or position is right for you. When you consider involving yourself in a relationship, you can determine whether or not the relationship contributes to the fulfillment of your mission. Your mission statement, written down and read regularly, helps give clarity to your everyday life. Decisions become easier to make. Bad situations suddenly become more obvious and you feel a pressing need to either fix those bad situations or let them go altogether. Creating your mission statement is not a difficult process, but it is a revealing one. To write a mission statement that is truly your own, you must listen to the innermost part of your being. What does your inner voice tell you it needs for complete fulfillment?

A mission is about more than the job you want or the size you would like your bank account to grow to. If you base your life's mission on "things," then you have no life purpose when those things go away. You should never define yourself by your job, by the company you own or work for, by the house you live in, or by your relationships with others. Your mission deals with your philosophy of life, your standards, and how you go about living. Your mission should not only incorporate your own desires for living, but also it should describe how your life impacts those whom you encounter. I thoroughly enjoyed the process of defining my personal mission. Now I read it regularly and strive to live it every day. I have several tiny copies of my mission statement strategically displayed in places where I know I will view them every day—in the corner of my bathroom mirror, on the printer that sits on my desk in my office, and inside the front cover of my day planner. It reads:

Valorie's Personal Mission Statement

To create and enjoy a fulfilling, prosperous, and charitable life, and to inspire others to do the same.

Valorie Burton

Create Your Mission Statement

By following a few simple guidelines, you can create a personal mission statement of your own. Start with what you want to accomplish through your everyday activities. Notice that I used the word "through." That is important to note, because your mission should and can be accomplished through many different activities. It should be transferable from one job, project, responsibility, or activity to another. If your mission statement only allows you to carry out your mission in one specific way, then it is not transferable. It does not allow you the flexibility to change course.

"My mission is to be promoted to vice-president within the next three years" is not transferable and it does not explain how your mission will benefit anyone else. This statement is a wonderful goal, but as a mission it is inadequate. Let's take another look at my personal mission statement and discover how it is transferable to all areas of my life.

To create and enjoy a fulfilling, prosperous, and charitable life, and to inspire others to do the same.

First, my mission is action-oriented. The action is described by three verbs: "create," "enjoy," and "inspire." I can do all three of these things in various areas of my life—through my entrepreneurial endeavors, writing, speaking engagements, and one-on-one with family, friends, clients, and people that I don't even know. My primary concerns are to create a life that is fulfilling, prosperous, and charitable; to enjoy the life that I create for myself; and, last but not least, to inspire others to live in a similar way. I am able to live my mission by pursuing my dreams and using the gift of communication to inspire others to pursue theirs and enjoy the rich rewards that come from living the lives they truly want to live.

Your personal mission statement should be short, to the point, action-oriented, and entirely your own. You cannot live out the mission that someone else thinks you should have for yourself. It must be *yours.* Your mission will fit you like a glove. Living your mission gives you joy. In fact, you are probably living your mission, at least to some degree, right now. You just haven't pinpointed it in writing.

Begin with active verbs that describe what you want to do

through your life. Use one to three verbs. Consider the following verbs, or any others that fit your mission:

Accomplish	Affect	Affirm
Appreciate	Build	Choose
Communicate	Compete	Complete
Complement	Continue	Counsel
Create	Cultivate	Defend
Deliver	Demonstrate	Discover
Discuss	Educate	Encourage
Enhance	Enjoy	Enlighten
Enrich	Entertain	Explore
Express	Facilitate	Finance
Generate	Give	Heal
Identify	Impact	Implement
Improve	Inspire	Invest
Lead	Live	Love
Measure	Mold	Motivate
Nurture	Open	Organize
Perform	Practice	Praise
Promote	Provide	Pursue
Receive	Renew	Respect
Satisfy	Save	Sell
Serve	Share	Speak

Rich Minds, Rich Rewards

Support	Sustain	Touch
Travel	Understand	Use
Value	Volunteer	Win
Work	Write	

In Part One of your personal mission statement, identify three verbs that describe the action of your mission. My personal mission is to _____, _____, and _____.

Part Two of your mission statement deals with the purpose, philosophy, cause, principle, or value that is most important to you. The appropriate word or phrase belongs in Part Two. Feel free to add adjectives, as I have in my personal mission statement, to describe the word or phrase, if it will make the mission statement clearer for you. Write the word or phrase here: _____.

In Part Three, choose the group or cause you desire to affect in a positive way. Write it here: _____. With words for all three parts, you now have the recipe for your mission statement. Let's put them all together.

Part One: To _____

_____

Valorie Burton

Part Two: _____

_____

Part Three: [to, for, or with] _____

_____ .

As needed, you can rearrange your mission statement so that it communicates to you in the clearest way possible. Just make sure that your personal mission statement includes all three parts and remains to the point. Put your mission statement in a place (or places) where you will see it every day. Use this space to write your completed mission statement:

My Personal Mission Statement:

_____

_____

_____ .

Have a Vision

The achievement of a goal always begins with a vision. Proverbs 29:18 tells us, "Where there is no vision, the people perish." A vision is what drives you as you carry out your mission. Your vision is the "ideal" of where you want to be. While your mission explains *why* you should do what you do, your vision explains *how.* It is the end result of your efforts. Success begins with vision. It is the destination on your life's road map. If you have a vision for your life, then you always know where you are going. You may get off track along the way. You might make a few wrong turns, but you never get completely lost because you have vision for where you are headed.

What is your vision? What does your ideal life look like? Your vision is an element of your life that must be clear, specific, and compelling enough that you will strive to attain it even when times are difficult. Your vision should motivate you to keep moving forward. Your vision should be a present-tense statement of what life will be at a given date in the future. When you state your vision, you should state it as though it has already happened, as if you are living it *now*. Your vision is that you have already accomplished what you are setting out to do. So write your vision statement as you envision life in your ideal world. The vision statement should include the various activities you will be involved in as you live your vision. Do not leave anything out, if it is part of what you envision. Everything that you visualize in your mind should be written in the present tense on paper. Don't rely on your memory. Include your ideal time frame and a detailed description. Unlike your mission statement, your vision statement should not consist of one succinct sentence.

Your vision statement describes verbally the vision for your mind. The more detailed your vision, the more real it becomes to you. It is no longer an abstract dream. When you vividly describe your vision, it excites your mind so much that you can almost feel it, taste it, hear it, and smell it. It becomes real to you. And once something becomes real to you, you believe that you can have it. In fact, you can! It's yours for the taking. All you have to do is take the right steps down the path that leads you to the vision.

When you get off track or make a wrong turn, your vision statement can be a compass that guides you back to the right path.

Create a Vision Statement

Imagine for a moment that you are living your ideal life right now. Everything that you see in your vision for the future is taking place right now, in the present. Describe what your day-to-day life looks like over the course of a typical week. This is your preliminary vision statement:

_____

_____

_____

_____

_____

Does your preliminary vision statement carry out your mission? Hopefully so. If not, you should first reevaluate your mission and ask yourself if your mission is authentic and based on your innermost desires. If you are positive that your mission is authentic, next look closely at your vision statement. What do you find in your preliminary vision statement that does not match up with your stated mission? How could you enhance your preliminary vision statement so that it complements your mission statement? In order to find fulfillment in every area of your life—career, personal, and spiritual—your mission must complement your vision, and vice versa.

The following is an example of a mission statement and vision statement of a parent who is a schoolteacher. It illustrates the vision for how a mission will be accomplished on a day-to-day basis.

Mission: To create, nurture and promote a loving, learning environment for myself and those around me.

Vision: I teach math to fifth-graders in an elementary school where the administration is supportive of its teachers and considers the successful education of its students its top priority. I am a loving parent of two children. I tell them that I love them often. I treat my colleagues and the members of my family well. I share a loving, communicative marriage with my spouse. We are great friends, go on a date once a week, and are affectionate with one another. On alternating nights my spouse and I take turns helping the girls with their homework. We lead by example by limiting the amount of television we watch, and we monitor the shows that we allow them to watch. I facilitate non-academic learning by involving the girls in sports that they enjoy and by exposing them to the arts. Once each month, we attend a play, concert, museum exhibit, or dance performance. Once each semester, I do the same with my students as a field trip.

Notice how the vision spells out the specifics for how the mission is to be carried out? Look at your preliminary vision statement again. Could it be more specific? See if you can improve upon your preliminary vision statement. Write your revised vision statement here. Continue on the next page if necessary.

_____

_____

_____

_____

_____

_____

_____

_____

_____

Valorie Burton

Write Down Your Goals

One of the first things I learned in business is that there is power in the written word. I found that I could verbally explain a marketing or public relations idea to my boss and she would listen. But if I took the time to type out my idea, print it, and then present it, the idea would receive more attention. Writing it down seemed to make it more official. The same principle holds true when it comes to the goals you are going to achieve. You should go one step beyond just carrying your goals and ideas around in your head. Make your goals official by writing them down. Often when you do not write a goal down, it remains a vague dream that you plan to accomplish at some undetermined date in the future. To move your goals from dream to reality, begin by writing them down. You've heard people (or maybe yourself) say things like "One day I'm going to do such and such," or "I plan to do that someday."

This kind of language clearly indicates that the person has

not begun to think about when or how she will reach her goal. In my own life, I have found that figuring out when and how has been a wonderful catalyst for moving me to action. My excitement builds as I construct a plan for reaching the goal. Most of the fun is in the process of getting to your destination. So let's begin your process by writing your goals down. Write down three goals that you would like to reach. Think big!

Goal 1: _____

Time Frame _____

Goal 2: _____

Time Frame _____

Goal 3: _____

Time Frame _____

Now, beginning with goal number 1, write down the steps you need to take to reach your goal. What things need to happen in order for you to make each dream a reality?

Goal 1: _____

_____

Valorie Burton

Things that must happen to make this dream a reality:

_____

_____

_____

_____

Goal 2:_____

_____

Things that must happen to make this dream a reality:

_____

_____

_____

_____

Goal 3:_____

_____

Things that must happen to make this dream a reality:

_____

_____

_____

_____

Keep a "goal journal" so that you can elaborate on your goals and jot down ideas as they come to you. As you move toward reaching each of your goals, refer to what you have written and see if you are on track. By breaking your larger goals into smaller ones, you make the process of reaching each goal more manageable. Your focus will be on successfully completing each step that leads toward the goal. Therefore, you can celebrate the success of continually moving closer to the goal. It all begins with you writing down your goals and making them official.

Your goal journal will be a helpful tool. As you come up with new ideas and revise your goal, it serves as a notebook that is completely dedicated to your goals. As you write down each goal, questions will come to mind about how to reach it and what you will need to do to achieve it. When you write your goals down, you have the freedom and the motivation to be very specific about what you want. As you get more specific, the details of a plan of action will become clear. It is so important to be specific about what you want. If you are not specific, you may find yourself putting your time and energy into activities that do not lead you to accomplish what you want most. So take your time when you are writing your goals down, listen to your inner voice, and make sure your goals are all your own.

Don't Downsize Your Dream

Fear manifests itself in many ways. If you have identified your most desired goal yet you find yourself pursuing it only indirectly, then you have allowed fear to step in and downsize your dream. Instead of fearlessly pursuing the goal, you have settled for doing something that perhaps draws on similar skills and is easier to pursue. The world is filled with English teachers who have dreamed of writing novels but never took that first step. Instead, they work in a profession that requires them to teach about novels, read novels, and teach students the basics of writing. Yet they never use those skills to fulfill a lifelong dream of being a novelist.

There are hundreds of agents, radio DJs, and A&R reps whose real desire was to be a performer, but instead of pursuing the goal of being a performer, they chose a profession that would enable them to be near performers. Not to pick on English teachers or people in the music business, but these examples illustrate the point. Be true to yourself. Pursue your true goal and don't beat around the bush when it comes to your dreams. When you know what you really want, go after it directly. It is okay to do something else to "pay the bills" while you are pursuing your goal, but don't downsize your dream. Always pursue the number-one goal.

Valorie Burton

Take the First Step

I am convinced that one of the biggest reasons why people never reach their goals is because they spend far too much time analyzing, contemplating, planning, and weighing the risks. Instead of taking the plunge, they test the waters by standing at the edge of the pool and sticking their big toe in. Well, the fact of the matter is that you don't learn how to swim by "testing the waters"! You have to take the plunge and get in the water. That's the first step. It can be a little scary when you take that first step toward your goal. The part of your brain that second-guesses your decisions will kick into overdrive. All kinds of questions will creep in. What if I'm not good enough? Should I plan a little bit more? What was I thinking when I came up with this idea? And the list goes on. Don't let these questions dissuade you. The first step is the most significant, because it sets everything into motion. I will never forget the fear that I felt when I decided to open my public relations agency. The first and scariest step was turning in my letter of resignation to my employer and letting them know that I would be leaving to start my own company. I knew that once I handed over that letter, there would be no turning back. I had taken the plunge. I wasn't swimming yet, but I definitely wasn't just testing the waters anymore. Without that first step, my life would be quite different today. That old saying is true: "The journey of a thousand miles begins with the first step."

Feel the Fear and
Don't Let It Stop You!

Sometimes taking that first step toward your goal and feeling scared go hand in hand. You know where you want your steps to lead, but there is no absolute guarantee that you will get there. Fear originates in thoughts of negative outcomes. We are afraid of what might happen if things do not go as we would like.

When I was on the brink of starting my business, an element of fear set in. All of these awful "what if" questions kept coming to mind. "What if my business fails?" "What if companies don't want to hire me?" "What if I need experience working for a PR agency first?" I made a very important decision about my "what if" questions. I decided to answer them. Answering your own questions is usually one of the best things that you can do to eliminate—or at least reduce—your level of fear. Here's what it looked like when I started answering my own questions.

First question: What if my business fails?

Answer: Well, I guess that means I'll have to find another job.

Consequence: I go back to working for someone else.

Second question: What if no one wants to hire me?

Answer: Valorie, you're starting the business with two clients. As you build your reputation, you will also build your client base. If no one wants to hire you, then you've got your answer to the first question . . . find a job.

Consequence: I go back to working for someone else.

Third question: What if I really need to get some more experience first and I just don't know it?

Answer: You'll never know everything. You can gain experience as you go, and for areas where you don't have the expertise needed, hire someone who does. If you didn't know what you were doing, no one would be coming to you to help with their marketing and public relations efforts. They believe in you. Now you just need to do the same.

Consequence: Get more experience. Get help from someone with more experience. There doesn't seem to be a negative consequence to this particular fear question.

After answering the negative questions that persisted in my head and created my fear, I realized that at the core of it

Valorie Burton

all, I was afraid that the business might fail. If the business failed, I would have to go out and find a job. Well, that certainly did not seem to be anything to be afraid of. After all, at that point in time, I had a great job at a friendly company, and although I had an entrepreneurial spirit, I was pretty happy with the job. Perhaps the thing that my fear was rooted in had more to do with the idea that my ego might get bruised if I started a business and it failed. I made the choice to deal with that consequence if and when it ever happened.

We can combat fear by focusing on positive outcomes. When you feel an element of fear creeping into your mind, begin visualizing the positive results and rewards of reaching your goal. It is crucial that you learn to do this because fear can never completely be eliminated from our lives. It is natural and it is normal. It is a human emotion. We should expect to feel fear. We simply have to deal with it and keep moving forward. By learning to focus on the positive outcome of reaching a goal rather than the negative outcome of falling short of it, we are able to control our fear and keep it from creating imaginary obstacles on our path to success. I have had my business since the end of 1996 and I still feel fear. I think that many entrepreneurs are motivated to succeed by the fear of failure. What a great example of turning a negative into a positive!

Let Go and Let God

Unfortunately, fear is often accompanied by its pesky, counterproductive sibling, worry. While fear is a natural emotion that you should allow to run its course, worry should be nipped in the bud. Constant worry indicates a lack of faith and a need for spiritual growth. The Bible even describes worry as a sin. Philippians 4:6 says, "Do not worry about anything, but in everything, by prayer and petition, with thanksgiving, present your requests to God." In other words, no matter what the situation, pray about it, ask for God's help, be thankful and gracious in doing so, and then have faith. Through faith you exercise patience. Through faith you believe that things will work out as they should, not necessarily as *you* think they should, but as God thinks they should. This kind of faith requires you to "let go and let God."

An important part of living a fulfilling and successful life is understanding and accepting that we simply do not have control over every outcome. There is a power greater than we are. Some things that happen (or do not happen) in life we will never be able to understand. Our job is to do our best with what we can control. If you pay attention and work on the things that you can control, you will have much less to worry about anyway.

For example, if you are a student and exams are a major source of worry in your life, then arrange your academic life so that when exam time comes, you are prepared. This will probably require a change in your study habits and perhaps a few adjustments to your social life, but if you arrange it right, you will find a balance that serves your needs and eliminates your worrying when exam time rolls around. If you are in a work situation that has you worried, it is vital to your quality of life that you find some way to deal with the issues. Many of us spend so much of our lives working that it is vitally important for us to be at peace in our work lives. First and foremost, you should like what you do. Going to a job that makes you sick, literally or figuratively, is detrimental to your health and creates an abundance of worry. If you find yourself in this type of situation, begin exploring your options. Remember that everything in life is a choice. Do not choose to live with a job that makes you sick with worry. You deserve more than that.

Some "worry" situations are beyond our control. During

these times, it can be more difficult not to worry. These are the frightening times in our lives when negative situations that are beyond our control affect our health or the health of a loved one, our finances, our family, or our environment. These are the times when our faith is tested. These are the times when we should do everything in our power to help the situation and pray for what is beyond our power. Then let go and let God.

———————

Valorie Burton

Use Failure as a Learning Tool

In a commencement address to graduates of Wellesley College in 1997, Oprah Winfrey said: "Failure is God's way of saying, 'Excuse me, you are moving in the wrong direction.' " Failing at something doesn't make you a failure. There is a lot to be learned from failing that can help you to succeed.

Sometimes the thing that we put our effort into is not the thing that we were destined to be doing. By failing, we are forced to try something new. And that something new just might be our calling—it might be the one thing in our lives where our effort to succeed doesn't feel like effort at all. It is so comfortable and comes so naturally that doing it is like breathing. That is how Oprah describes her very first day hosting a talk show in the late 1970s. "I knew that was what I was supposed to be doing," she said.

While failure is not a pleasant experience, I am very thankful for many of my failures. I call them "power failures," because the failures I have faced have empowered me to move in a new direction. Without them, I would be living a completely different life right now. My "power failures" have forced me in new directions that have led to wonderful successes.

One of the first that comes to mind is my first year of college. It was no ordinary experience to say the least. I had an extremely difficult time coming to terms with the sense of failure I felt when I decided to "punch out" after nearly a year as a cadet at the U.S. Air Force Academy. It took me years to see that I had not failed. Instead, I had learned a great deal about myself that I otherwise would not have at such a young age. Nonetheless, during that year, I lost an enormous amount of academic confidence. It was actually quite an irony. I had been a strong enough candidate to receive a presidential appointment to attend the Air Force Academy, yet I spent almost the entire school year on academic probation. That, along with three stays in the hospital, an adjustment to military protocol, and my parents' divorce did not make for the most pleasant year of my life. I am grateful for that year, though. I learned more from that year than I had in the previous eighteen years of my life.

For one thing, I learned that what you think you want in

life may look fabulous until you actually start doing it. I thought I knew that the Academy was for me. Once I became a cadet, however, I quickly realized that I did not share the passion for flying and military life that many of my fellow classmates had. I loved the friends that I made while I was there. I knew what an honor it was to be there. I admired the legacy of the people who had walked that campus before me. But outside factors like those did not fuel a passion in my heart. I believe that it was in God's plan for me to go to the Air Force Academy and it was in His plan for me to leave. Had I enjoyed a successful career at the Academy, I know in my heart that I would not have left. It took failure to move me in a new direction.

Where did that new direction lead? Well, it led me on a journey that continues today in a fulfilling life as an entrepreneur, writer, and speaker. I have no regrets. I can see clearly now that everything happens for a reason. Failing in the pursuit of a dream can lead you to your true destiny.

Name one instance in which you really wanted to succeed, but you failed. _____

_____

_____

_____

In what new direction or success did you move after the failure? _____

_____

_____

_____

What positive things resulted from this "power failure"?____

_____

_____

_____

―――――――――

Do What You Love
and the Rewards Will Come

The best advice one of my mentors ever gave me was that I should do what I love and the rewards will come. The first time he said it, I thought that it sounded a little too idealistic. But as I have grown spiritually, mentally, and emotionally, I have found his words to be absolutely true.

Why? Because if you love your work, you'll put your heart and mind into doing your job well. You'll be more creative. You'll have more energy to do your work. You'll seek to learn more and grow in your career. Because you are enthusiastic, your employer will take notice, or your customers will take notice. Soon you will get better assignments, perhaps a promotion. Your customers will refer business your way and do more business with you. The possibilities are endless. You see, when you do what you love, you find ways to create new opportunities for yourself, sometimes without even realizing that is what you are doing.

After I was promoted to marketing director for a leading Dallas accounting firm, Lane Gorman Trubitt, L.L.P., I began to come up with new ideas for the firm's marketing push. My efforts resulted in news articles being written about the firm and some well-received events that the firm sponsored to boost our name recognition in the business community. Other companies took notice and a couple of them called me and asked if I might be interested in doing some public relations work on the side. One of the opportunities that came along gave me an opening to actually start my own business. That was in late 1996. After a couple of months of contemplation, I made the leap and launched my PR firm, The Burton Agency, the month I turned twenty-four. In doing so, I was fortunate enough to be able to begin a client relationship with my former employer. I am convinced that my love for journalism and public relations is what led me to such a quick path to entrepreneurship.

Let's consider the path I'm talking about. While a junior at Florida State University, I saw in an ad in the student newspaper that the governor's office was looking for public relations interns. Although my major was international affairs, I decided to call and inquire. I was interviewed and offered the internship. I liked it a lot; the pace was fast and the things we dealt with were exciting and important. I had the chance to

Valorie Burton

write and learned quite a bit as a result. I rediscovered my interest in journalism, which I had once considered for a major. Upon graduation from FSU less than a year later, I chose to enter graduate school and earn a master's degree in journalism at Florida A&M University. My love for communications became even more evident as I devoured the subject matter and began working in media relations for a new minor-league hockey team in Tallahassee. My enthusiasm led to more responsibility and some great assignments, like reporting on the team's local TV show. I finished graduate school a little over a year later.

I moved to Dallas and began as a marketing assistant at Lane Gorman. When my boss left the firm, I believe it was the master's degree that I had enthusiastically pursued, coupled with my ideas and enthusiasm for the open position, that helped me land the promotion to marketing director after only four months with the firm.

If I had been moving along in a career field I didn't enjoy, going through the motions, I would not have shown much enthusiasm and creativity. And, most likely, I would not have been promoted. If I had not been promoted to marketing director, I would not have had the opportunity to do the types of things that attracted attention and led me to start The Burton Agency. Each step of the way, the rewards have been numerous. There is no question in my mind that if you do what you love, the rewards will come. It is a principle that reminds me of a piece of advice Kenny Rogers says he got from his mother: "Do what you love and you'll never work a day in your life."

Valorie Burton

To Do Your Best Work,
Be Your Best Self

If you have ever been an athlete, you know that doing your best requires a comprehensive approach to preparation. A track star must do more than practice running. To win convincingly and consistently, she must be at her best in every area that affects her performance. Of course, talent and speed are essential, but muscle strength, endurance, nutrition, and a winning attitude all play a major role as well. Speed without endurance won't win in the long run. And she can be prepared in every other area, but if in her mental attitude she lacks the belief that she can win, then she probably won't. In track, like so many competitive ventures, it is the work a runner does on the inside that matters most. It's the nutrition she puts in her body, the muscle strength she builds, the capacity for endurance she develops, and the rich mind that believes she can do it. It is this inner work that gives her the competitive advantage.

I have discovered this concept to be true in every area of life: In order to *do* your best work, you need to *be* your best self. That is why it is critical to continually seek ways to enrich, enhance, and empower your mind. The power to succeed begins within. Whatever your mind believes, will manifest itself in your outside world.

It is impossible to produce fresh, sweet orange juice from a rotten orange. The same principle holds true for us as individuals. To produce our best work, we must be willing to hold a mirror to our inner lives and see what work needs to be done. All types of inner issues can keep you from being your best self. Which ones do you sometimes find yourself dealing with?

- Negative attitude
- Lack of confidence
- Jealousy
- Anger or bitterness
- Fear
- Procrastination
- Lack of knowledge or skills

When any of these issues are present, they negatively affect you—first inwardly, and then they project outwardly into

Valorie Burton

your career, love relationships, friendships, finances, or spiritual life.

So how do you become your best self? By prioritizing your life and committing yourself to that which brings you joy and fulfillment. Becoming your best self also means dealing with past issues, clearing your mental and emotional clutter, and replacing negative habits with positive ones.

Being your best self is a state of continual improvement. As we learn and grow, our best gets better. Life is a journey of experiences that become life lessons. We continually learn, therefore we continually have the opportunity for our best self to get even better.

Personal PR

As a public relations professional, I understand the value of image building and effective communication. The same principles that work to make businesses successful can help you with your own personal career success. The following is adapted from a column I wrote that appeared in the *Dallas Business Journal.* It illustrates my point.

Isn't it interesting that some of the most successful business people aren't necessarily the ones who have the most experience or education in their chosen field? Instead, they are often the ones with the best people skills. They are thoughtful, trustworthy, dependable, and easy to work with. In essence, they are pros at "personal PR" (public relations).

Take for example, PR guru Terrie Williams. In 1988, she opened the doors of what would become one of the nation's leading entertainment PR firms. Her first two clients? Eddie

Valorie Burton

Murphy and Miles Davis. Not bad for a woman with no PR agency experience and a master's degree in social work. How did she do it? According to Terrie's book, *The Personal Touch: What You Really Need to Succeed in Today's Fast-Paced Business World,* it was not so much her professional abilities (although superb) but her personal PR skills that led to her entrepreneurial success.

Building a business from the ground up is no easy feat. But the challenge can be both fun and rewarding. Whether you are an entrepreneur or a salesperson, the importance of effective personal communication with your customers, prospects, and referral sources is essential. All of the advertising and public relations in the world can be great for bringing in customers, but if the personal PR skills of the individuals at the company are lacking, you'll drive those same customers away. From the CEO to the receptionist, everyone has an impact on the image that people perceive of your company. After all, a company is only as strong as its people.

Remember that when you communicate it's the little things that can have the most significant impact. Do your personal PR skills make you stand out from the competition? If the answer to that question isn't immediately clear, then maybe it's time to sharpen those skills. Here are some ways that you can begin to do just that:

- **Return all phone calls.** Not only is this common courtesy, but if you are a professional, this is an essential.
- **Don't blow people off.** You never know where contacts made today can lead to tomorrow. You may regret blowing off someone with whom you could have a mutually beneficial relationship down the road.
- **Send thank-you notes.** This is quick and easy, and, most important, people appreciate it. A verbal thank-you is fine, but why not follow up with a written thank-you as well?
- **Don't make a habit of complaining.** Try to make the best of every situation by remaining positive.
- **Be knowledgeable about your profession.** Stay abreast of trends in your profession. Network with others in your profession so that you are a resource to them and they can be a resource to you. These types of relationships can sometimes lead to profitable strategic alliances.
- **Write.** Send letters, postcards, articles, newsletters, and other correspondence to keep in touch with people you've met and whom you want to remember you. Write letters or notes to people you've read about or heard give a speech.
- **Be dependable.** If you say that you will do something, do it. And if you simply can't, say so, and come up with an alternative.

Valorie Burton

- **Listen.** Make a habit of being interested in what people have to say. Listen to them before making a point of being heard.

- **Speak to groups and organizations.** Brush up on your public-speaking skills or consider joining a group such as Toastmasters International. Public speaking, when done well, can be a very positive PR tool.

- **Treasure your reputation.** Your reputation is your most valuable asset. Build a strong one and guard it closely by treating people with respect, and by delivering good customer service and a quality product.

- **Get involved.** Give back in some tangible way through volunteering or serving in the community in some capacity. This involvement could include the arts, non-profit organizations, youth groups, chambers of commerce, or other community organizations.

Save the Drama

Do you remember when you were in high school and the slightest incident between certain people became the hottest news in an instant? Everyone talked about it, recounting every detail and blowing everything completely out of proportion. By the time the news filtered through several layers of people, it was a different story entirely. And then the cycle would start all over again. *Drama!* Some adults still live their day-to-day lives like this. Every little thing is a big deal. They never have peace in their lives because something is always stirring. Everything that happens in their relationships must be analyzed, dissected, and offered up for an opinion from people who shouldn't know all of their business to begin with.

Dramatics, as I like to call them, are gossips. They make an issue out of stuff that doesn't even affect them. They are concerned about who Angela, who sits three cubicles away, is

Valorie Burton

talking to at lunch, and that what James wore on casual day is too casual. Dramatics, let it go! Why be concerned and stressed over stuff that really doesn't affect you?

Now, when it comes to those situations that actually affect dramatics, the drama can get pretty much out of hand. The smallest problem can ruin an otherwise perfect day. It seems that dramatics blow everything out of proportion. Well, we all have our moments. And we have all had moments when we could have been classified as a dramatic. The key is to recognize that you are blowing a situation out of proportion and stop the snowball effect before it goes too far. One technique is to take several deep breaths and try to put everything into perspective before taking any action or saying anything aloud.

I find myself in dramatic mode sometimes when I am managing an event. Inevitably something does not go according to my plan. The florist doesn't deliver enough centerpieces for all of the tables, a celebrity misses her flight, a star athlete shows up an hour late, or the audiovisual equipment fails in the middle of a presentation. All of these scenarios have occurred in the midst of events I was managing. What did I do? Well, quite honestly, on a couple of occasions I panicked and the snowball was in full effect. Then I stopped for a moment. I took a few deep breaths, put on my thinking cap,

Rich Minds, Rich Rewards

and came up with a Plan B—and fast! Creating a lot of drama around these situations would not have changed the circumstances. Things don't always happen the way that we would like. Sometimes you just have to save the drama and go with the flow.

Valorie Burton

Say Please and Thank You

One of the best ways to make friends, keep friends, and maintain an environment of appreciation in both your personal and career life is to be gracious. A column that I wrote for the *Dallas Business Journal* in early 1997 sums up my advice on saying "please" and "thank you." Here it is:

"Lessons for Adults Come from Mouths of Babes"
(*Dallas Business Journal*, Feb. 21–27, 1997)

Those of you with young children may be able to answer this question: Why do children watch the same videotape 600 times before moving on to a new one? For some reason, it seems they have to memorize the entire tape before they will take it out of the VCR.

I don't have any children, but my only sibling is three and a half years old. (No, that's not a typo—we're more than two decades apart.) It amazes me that at such a young age, he has mastered Sega, the remote control, and, for two years now, the VCR. So it won't surprise you that I have spent countless hours in front of the tube watching the same Barney videos over and over and over and . . . well, you get the picture.

I can blame only myself. After all, Wade got his first Barney video as a Christmas present from—guess who? His big sister. I dreaded sitting and watching the big purple dinosaur with the goofy voice. To be blunt, Barney annoyed me. And to make matters worse, I would occasionally find myself driving around town with songs like "I Love You, You Love Me" playing in my head. This certainly didn't make me like Barney any more. But today I'm not so hard on the big guy.

First of all, he's not supposed to entertain me. He's supposed to entertain little kids. And, secondly, he has a pretty good message. Stick with me. I'm going somewhere with this. Lucky for me, my brother is apparently "Barney-ed out." He moved on to animated characters like Snoopy and Bambi about six months ago. Poor Barney has been collecting dust on the video shelf. But last week when I stopped by for a visit, Wade was watching Barney and his entourage of children crooning "Please and Thank You, They're the Magic Words," one of Barney's greatest hits.

I got to thinking. You know, it wouldn't hurt for some

Valorie Burton

adults to pick up on the purple dinosaur's message. I often wonder what has happened to our manners. These days, courtesy seems to be the exception rather than the rule. Sad, isn't it? No matter where I go, I seem to run into rude people. I was recently driving on the freeway when a woman who had begun to exit the freeway changed her mind at the last moment and decided to get back onto the freeway. I thought that she was going to hit me, so I blew my horn. I could be optimistic and say she waved to thank me for letting her in, but she didn't wave her whole hand, just one finger.

In our fast-paced world of impersonal communication—fax, voice mail, e-mail—courtesy and appreciation seem to be falling by the wayside. Remember just a couple of years ago when you called "411" and the operator said, "Good evening. What city, please?" Now she's only allowed to say, "What city?" Omitting the three extra courtesy words apparently shaves off an extra two seconds from each phone call, thereby creating more efficiency. Well, at least the phone company has a reason. I don't *like* their reason, but at least they have one, which is more than I can say for numerous others with whom I come in contact every day.

So often a smile, coupled with a simple "please" or "thank you" can take you a long way. If you aren't already doing these, here are some ideas:

- Set aside fifteen minutes each week to write thank-you notes to people who have gone out of their way for you.
- When you see a company or person you know in the newspaper, take time to send a note of congratulations.
- Say "please" to people who work for and with you, not just the people for whom you work.
- At your own company or when you are visiting one, be as courteous to the receptionist as you are to the president.
- Tell your employees when they're doing a good job.
- Say "thank you."

Valorie Burton

Express Love

In our fast-paced, high-tech world, opportunities are too often missed to express love for others. But when you evaluate your life, your success should be based on the most essential element: love. Giving love to others symbolizes your ability to experience joy in your life. Think back on the experiences in your life that have brought you the most joy. Most likely, those experiences were ones that involved people in your life whom you love and care about. Negative experiences in the area of relationships with loved ones can stifle your joy. If we are hurt by those to whom we have shown our love, a natural reaction can be to withdraw our expressions of love for fear that we will be hurt again. But doing so is far more detrimental to you than it is to those on the receiving end of your love. Why? Because when your door of love is open to give, it is also open to receive. Everyone, at the core of his or her being, wants to be loved. So let those around you know that you love them. And do your best to love them unconditionally. Your love should be a gift, not a bartering tool.

Love can be expressed in many ways. Love can be expressed in the tone of your voice during conversation. Love can be expressed through encouraging words to a co-worker who is having a difficult time. Love can be expressed through a friendly smile to a stranger. Love can be expressed when you hug a friend. Love can be expressed in a handwritten note thanking someone you care about for just being who they are. Love can be expressed when you tell the important people in your life that you love them. Tell your children you love them. Tell your family. Tell your friends. We should love people for being who they are to us, not just for doing what they do for us. And we should not take for granted that people know exactly how we feel. To be sure, we should tell them.

Valorie Burton

Mind Your Own Business

This book is about elevating your mind and focusing inward to uncover your dreams and then exercising the courage to reach them. The focus of each mini-chapter is on *you*. Even if the end result of acting on the advice in each mini-chapter ultimately affects other people, everything in this book is about the choices *you* make that lead to your ability to live a fulfilled and personally successful life. So don't get caught up in what others are doing in their lives as it compares to yours. This type of comparison often occurs in a competitive situation. We become so focused on someone else's actions and achievements (or lack thereof) that we lose sight of our own. Your time and energy is very valuable. Spend it on you!

I discovered this type of wasted energy when I was competing in pageants, and I was quite guilty myself until I became a more mature competitor. I would spend time sizing up the competition and watching them during rehearsals. My behavior was always counterproductive. What on earth was I accomplishing by concerning myself with someone else's performance? Absolutely nothing. In fact, I was losing valuable energy that I could have spent mentally preparing for my own performance. The fact is that we cannot control someone else's actions—how well they do or don't do at something. If you are in competition with someone—whether for a new client, a job, or even the title of Miss America—the most important thing to remember is that the only thing you need to concern yourself with is your own performance. If it is meant to be, it will be. If it isn't meant to be, make sure you find the life lesson in the experience of competing. Spend more time working on you and less time worrying about everybody else, and you'll be amazed at what you can accomplish.

Valorie Burton

Emulate Successful People

Making the decision to be fulfilled and successful doesn't mean that you need to reinvent the wheel. You are not the first person to find personal success and fulfillment, are you? Of course not! Use this fact to your advantage. Right now, take a moment to stop and think of one person whom you admire. Whether you know the person or not, think of someone who has achieved something similar to what you are striving for. Write his or her name here.

_____

Now make it your project to find out as much as you can about how that person accomplished what you are trying to accomplish. What is their background? How did they get started? What types of obstacles did they face? How did they overcome those obstacles? What is their education (formal or non-formal), and how does it relate to the goals that they have reached? It is very important to get answers to these questions because you can learn a great deal from the experiences of those who are successful in ways that you wish to be. If the person you named has a high profile, a little research in the library, at a local bookstore, or on the Internet is likely to result in an abundance of information, in the form of newspapers, magazines, and books. If the person is not high-profile but is someone that you know personally, take the time to ask her questions about how she came to find such success. Let the person know that you admire her and would appreciate her advice. Too often we fail to tell the people whom we admire most just how we feel. People are generally flattered by admiration and are quite willing to mentor those who would like to follow in their footsteps. Sometimes, the person who would be an excellent source of learning is a competitor. This is often true in business. In such cases, where mentoring is not an option, become an observant and perceptive learner. Just make sure that you find a balance between learning from your competitors and focusing on the things that you must do to improve yourself. You never want to lose sight of your own mission and vision.

Whatever your situation, don't attempt to reinvent strate-

Valorie Burton

gies for yourself. Many mistakes can be avoided by learning from the path that has already been traveled by other successful people. Emulate their success strategies and you may just find a shorter, less difficult, and more direct path to success.

Surround Yourself with People
Who Are Going Places

Once you make the decision to create a fulfilling, successful life and you begin to make changes in your life, two things may happen. First, you may experience resistance from some of your family and friends about your new attitude and outlook. For various reasons, some selfish and some well-intentioned, certain people will want you to stay right where you are. They may not want you to move ahead, because in their minds that could mean leaving them behind. Hopefully, this won't be the case in your life. If it is, be prepared. Stay strong. Hold on tightly to your dreams. And don't let anyone's negative reaction to what you are doing to improve your life discourage you to the point that you give up. Listen to your heart and do what is right for you.

The second thing that happens when you begin making changes to create a fulfilling and successful life is that you

Valorie Burton

begin to attract people into your life with a similar attitude. This is good. You should seek to attract positive people to your life—people who are going places. When you surround yourself with positive people, you develop mutually beneficial relationships that allow you to learn from others and vice versa. Your standards are higher because your frame of reference is better than average. If you find yourself in a situation where you are the most "together" of all your friends, co-workers, and other social groups, you need to look inward and ask yourself why. Do you feel more comfortable being the big fish in a little pond? Are you failing to challenge yourself in different areas of your life? Do you feel a need to always be the center of attention? Are you intimidated by those you perceive as being more successful than you are? If you answered "yes" to any of these questions, there is some "inner work" that you need to do to deal with insecurity. The most important thing to realize is that to reach your potential, you will have to step outside of your comfort zone into a "bigger domain." The people whom you encounter in this new domain can become a source of inspiration and encouragement. Seek these healthy relationships and learn to appreciate them.

By surrounding yourself with people whose outlook is similar to yours, you make it easier to maintain that outlook. It is not necessary for you to abandon all of your old ties. Explain yourself to friends and family. Encourage them to create the lives they truly want as well. If they are open to your encouragement, maintain a positive relationship with them. If not, stay positive and respect their decision. However, do not allow anyone to talk you out of your plans to create the fulfilling life you deserve.

Don't Make Excuses

When I was a cadet at the U.S. Air Force Academy, one of the best lessons that I learned is that the one thing that is inexcusable is an excuse. It has almost been a decade since I attended the Academy, and to this day I hate giving excuses for not doing something, even when the excuse is valid. In my mind, the bottom line is that the anticipated outcome did not come to pass. Who really cares about why it didn't happen? Adopt a "whatever it takes" attitude toward doing things that you tell people you will do. If an obstacle comes along that gets in the way, instead of quickly resolving that something cannot be done, look for a way to remove or go around that obstacle. Don't be quick to give up and use the obstacle as an excuse. Everyone faces obstacles. The key to success is learning to overcome them rather than using them as excuses for why you can't do the things you want to do.

Many of us have permanent (or semi-permanent) excuses for why we cannot do certain things. We express these excuses in statements such as, "If I had more money, I would start my own business" or "If I were married, I would buy a house" or "If I had a boyfriend, I would travel more." If you look at each of these statements again, you will recognize that the first half of the statement need not prevent the second half of the statement from actually occurring. The first half of the statement is nothing more than an excuse for not achieving the second half. You want to start a business and you need more money? You are not alone. Most people who start businesses don't start with a ton of money. They are creative and committed to the goal, so they find a way to overcome the obstacle of money. You want to buy your own place? Home ownership is not reserved for married couples. You don't have to wait for Prince Charming to sweep you off your feet and carry you over the threshold of your new home. That day will come, but unless you know for sure that it's right around the corner, why would you hold off investing in a piece of property for yourself if you have the means to do it? Along the same lines, if you like to travel, what are you waiting for? Take a trip by yourself. Go on vacation with friends. Don't put your life on hold waiting for "the one" to come along. You're worth the trouble all by yourself!

When you find yourself explaining to someone the reasons you can't do something, pause for a moment. Think about it. Then determine whether your reason is valid or if it is just an excuse that you are allowing to pose as an obstacle to getting something that you want. Instead of making an excuse, simply concede that whatever it is, you don't want it that badly. If it were really important to you, you would find a way to make it happen.

———————

Don't Play the Blame Game

Since we are already on the topic of not making excuses, let's talk about the blame game. Part of living a fulfilling life is learning to accept responsibility for our failures as much as we accept responsibility for our successes. When things don't go your way, avoid pointing the finger of responsibility at someone else. Don't blame other people for your problems. Their actions may have led to your current circumstances to one degree or another, but you have the power to stop blaming and rise above the circumstances. Always remember that your character is not measured by what happens to you, but by how you respond to what happens to you. When we blame people or circumstances for our situation, we are assigning ourselves "victim" status. Blaming robs us of time and energy. It causes us to harbor negative thoughts and focus on other people. Often, these "other people" aren't worth our time or energy. We need to move past the blaming

Valorie Burton

stage and use our time and energy in a positive way. Make a choice not to be a victim of the blame game. Make a choice to focus on the things that you can control. Make a choice to accept responsibility when you make a mistake. Make a choice to accept responsibility when you fail. Others will respect you for it, and so will you.

———————————

Focus on the Most
Important Task First

O ne of the biggest differences between those who are very successful and those who aren't has everything to do with how they spend their time. The inability to concentrate on the most important elements of reaching a particular goal can keep the most well-intentioned people from achieving success. They spend too much time and energy on things that are related to the ultimate goal, and although these things may be necessary, they do not constitute the most important piece of the project. In his book *Don't Worry, Make Money,* Richard Carlson refers to the most important piece of a goal as the "critical inch." The critical inch is the work that is most essential to achieving a given goal. For example, if you set out to write a book, there are many elements to the project that you will need to address before the book is actually ready to be distributed and sold. If you plan to sell it to a publisher,

Valorie Burton

you will probably need to find an agent, you will need to present a proposal with market research, develop a marketing strategy, and outline your chapters. If you decide to self-publish, there are a whole set of other issues you will need to deal with, such as establishing a publishing company, dealing with the printers, hiring someone to design the book, and so on. The critical inch of the project, however, is actually writing the book. Until you finish writing the book, you don't really have anything to market, sell, or publish.

Most of us have found ourselves in a predicament in which we have spent a great deal of time working on something yet it still appears that we have done very little. We get to the end of our workday and say to ourselves, "I was busy all day. Why is it that I still have so much left to do?" In many cases, we were busy, but not busy doing the things that mattered most. Instead, we were busy putting out little fires here and there, taking calls that were not as urgent as the tasks we needed to finish, and finding ways to procrastinate.

To begin tackling the critical inch, organize your efforts before you start working on a project. Ask yourself, "What is the core task of achieving my goal?" When you are able to identify what is truly important first, you become aware of the most important task at hand. You should then prioritize all of your tasks and concentrate on those at the top of your list first. If you find yourself doing other activities before you take care of the core task, you'll know that you are off track and probably procrastinating. Learn to concentrate on the core task and you'll find success more quickly than you ever thought possible.

Valorie Burton

Don't Try to Do Everything Yourself

Each one of us is blessed with specific gifts and talents. There are certain things that we are good at doing and certain things that we are good at being. No one, however, is good at everything. We can't possibly know everything. We cannot possibly do everything. Accepting your limitations can be a very freeing experience. It frees you to ask for help, and it can also free you from the headache and stress of trying to be all things at once. As a business owner, I have known this problem all too well at times. I have had to juggle numerous projects simultaneously while ensuring that clients are billed, the payroll and vendors are paid in a timely fashion, and, of course, that sales and business-development efforts never cease. The key to managing it all at once is knowing when and who to ask for help. Spending your valuable time and energy on necessary projects that you find both uninteresting and unfamiliar can negatively affect your ability to get done those things you find both interesting and familiar.

There are people who specialize in just about anything you might need help with—from accountants to seamstresses, administrative assistants to fitness trainers. Whatever it is that you need help with, there is someone out there who specializes in it. I am certainly not advocating that you shouldn't learn new skills or try something that is unfamiliar to you. I am simply suggesting that we should not try to do or be everything. To get more done, and get it done the right way, we should be willing to call on people who specialize in what we need.

By the same token, we should also seek out people who can serve as mentors, people we can go to when we have questions. These types of relationships can prove invaluable. There are formal mentoring programs you can take part in through your local chamber of commerce, as well as professional associations in your specific industry.

I have developed strong relationships with several friends who also have served as wonderful professional mentors. One of them has owned a major public relations agency and an advertising agency for thirty years. When I have questions dealing with new business development, he is there to give me his advice based on decades of experience building and running a successful agency. I have another mentor who is a former television reporter turned public relations director for a Fortune 500 company. His opinions on projects that my agency has created and produced have been extremely helpful. It is simply awesome how God puts people in our lives to help us and encourage us once we commit to a goal. When we work hard, get recognition for our efforts, and treat people well in the process, mentors and supporters seem to fall into place.

Get a Mentor

Whether you own your own business, work in corporate America, or are employed the public sector, a mentor can be incredibly helpful. A mentor is someone who is or has been where you are headed. As you chart new territory, it's nice to have someone to talk to and seek advice from who has already been where you are right now. They have wisdom that can be immensely useful to you, if you tap into it.

When I hear the term mentor, I am reminded of a hilarious episode of the sitcom *Seinfeld* in which Jerry was puzzled with his date's obsession with her "mentor." Having a mentor, she said was part of a strategy to "manage her career." Of course, Jerry questioned his date's choice of a mentor, once he learned that her mentor was dating his goofy, comedic nemesis, Banya. Jerry's date may have gone a little overboard with the "mentor-mentee" thing. Still, she had the right idea.

Many professionals, new and seasoned, don't plan their careers or find mentors to help them along. The ones who do, however, are one step ahead of the game. Young professionals, in particular, should follow five guidelines when establishing a career plan:

- Write down your life goals for the next one, five, and ten years. Tie those into your career goals. From those objectives, determine what you need to do to reach your goals.
- Set times to have a review with your boss to discuss your performance. Your review should be separate from time set aside for specific projects.
- Be clear on what needs to be accomplished to move up within the company.
- Rather than focusing exclusively on promotions, consider making lateral moves that will help you establish a broad base of experience.
- Don't be afraid to ask for what you want. You just might get it.

I interviewed two of my mentors, Ed Stewart and Sheilah Tucker, to see if they had any advice on the subject. As always, they did.

"Finding the right company is very important. Don't

look for the biggest company. Look for the best company for you," Ed told me. He is the director of public relations for Dallas-based Southwest Airlines. Ed left airline giant American Airlines for Southwest in 1990.

"Many people just couldn't understand why I would leave a bigger airline for a smaller one," he said. "In the end, it turned out to be the best career move of my life."

It is no surprise that he says that. In 1999, his department had the distinction of being named the best public relations department of any Fortune 500 company in the country. Ed credits his ability to manage the challenges of adversity and work successfully on high-visibility projects to his broad base of experience. He spent six years as a broadcast and print reporter before Southwestern Bell lured him to Dallas in 1984, a career change he had not anticipated.

"Flexibility is key," Ed said. "It's good to keep your eye on the prize, but sometimes you can't factor in all that might be thrown at you."

He also pointed out that young professionals should find someone to emulate. "I'm a strong believer in mentors," he told me. "Inevitably, there will be questions, and you need answers that you can trust. You need a mentor."

Sheilah Tucker agrees.

"Involve yourself in the types of activities that those

Valorie Burton

above you are involved in," she advised. Since 1992, Tucker has grown her firm ST & Associates Public Relations entirely through networking contacts. When I met Sheilah in 1995, I told her that I wanted to do what she does. She graciously advised and encouraged me when I went into business.

"It's all about meeting people and learning from their experiences," she said.

Sheilah stresses the importance of self-marketing. She tells young businesspeople to let those around them know of their interests, stay abreast of industry trends, and always be willing to learn.

"I didn't have anyone to teach me," she said of her first public relations job as PR director at ProLine Corporation. "I learned as much as I could because I had no other choice. I read everything I could find about public relations, and I listened."

Most important in the process of career planning, Ed emphasized, is a focus on fulfillment. "Career goals should be more than just monetary. You should focus on enhancing your life, because if you enjoy the work, the rewards will come."

Take a moment right now to identify one to three people who would be good mentors for you—people who are where you want to be in the future. If you don't know anyone personally, you can enlist what my pastor calls "historical mentors." Historical mentors are people—living or dead—whom you can study in books or audiovisual materials. Learn as much as possible through their experiences and apply the knowledge you learn to your career.

———————

Practice How You Want to Be

How often have you heard yourself say that you wanted to do something, but your actions led you in another direction? So often we dream about things that we would like to do or be, but we never actually start doing or being that thing. If you want to be less stressed, more patient, easier to get along with, or more healthy, then practice being that way. You become what you practice.

The old adage is true: "Practice makes perfect." Yet we continue to keep practicing what we don't want in our lives. We say that we want to become less stressed, but we keep doing things that contribute negatively to our stress level. We say that we want to lead a more fulfilling life, but we continue to practice being unfulfilled by doing the things that leave us empty and drained. We say that we want to be healthier but practice being unhealthy by continuing to eat poorly and exercising very little.

Becoming what you want most takes practice. The change won't happen overnight, but with practice, it happens. By practicing consistently, the habits that we want to form in our lives become second nature. Ask any professional athlete how they made it to the pros and they will tell you that intensive practice was a huge part of the equation. They had to practice being what they are now.

Practice is not only important when it comes to behaviors and habits such as being healthy, less stressed, or patient, but it is just as important when it comes to our life goals for career, family, relationships, and finances. If your goal is to land a certain position in the company that you work for, practice for it. Practice seeing the company from the point of view of someone already in that position. Broaden your vision of the company. Practice looking the part and acting the part. In doing so, you not only prepare yourself for the position, but you also enable others to envision you there. Once other people, particularly decision-makers, can envision you in the position, you are more than halfway to achieving your goal.

The same principle holds true in relationships. Being in a strong, loving, and mutually beneficial relationship takes practice. By practicing the habits you want to manifest in a relationship, you build the one that you want. If you want to receive love, then practice giving love. If you want to have more

Valorie Burton

fun, then practice being a fun person. If you don't want to bicker, then practice not needing to be right all the time. If you want romance, then practice being romantic. If you want to attract people into your life with these qualities, then practice these qualities in your own life. The people you attract to your life are a reflection of you and the habits you practice most.

The person that you are right now is a reflection of what you practice most. When you look in the mirror, what does your reflection say about the habits you practice? Do you reflect kindness? Hard work? Anger? Prosperity? Love? Patience? Be honest enough with yourself to see the good habits you should continue to practice, the bad habits you should cease to practice, and the missing habits you should begin to practice.

Take Control of Your Financial Life

Not too long ago I heard someone say that prosperity begins with the decision to prosper. The statement is simple, but so very true. People speak in such general terms about "someday" being comfortable, even wealthy. Yet their day-to-day actions indicate that the accumulation of wealth is at the bottom of their priority list. Although mired in debt, they continue to spend money they don't have while making minimum payments on credit-card bills for items they have used up or forgotten about long before. They don't maximize their investments, if indeed their money is invested at all. Worst of all, they live paycheck to paycheck, unable to handle financial emergencies or to go for any period of time without income from a job. Can you identify with any of these situations? If so, consider the following ideas for taking control of your financial life:

Make a decision to prosper. Commit to practicing behavior that will help you create a life of financial abundance. Make prosperity and the creation of wealth a priority in your life that governs the financial decisions you make. Adopt an entrepreneurial mindset and learn to spot and create wealth-building opportunities.

Believe that you are worthy of a financially abundant life. Do not allow your current or previous negative financial circumstances to trick you into believing that you do not deserve any more than you have right now. You deserve more and you can have more, if you practice and work at it.

Live below your means. One of the keys to living a financially prosperous life is to live below your means. Do not spend more than you can afford. Practice doing without things that you believe you "just have to have" for a while before buying them. Then if you still feel you "just have to have it," and you can afford it, buy it. Make a habit of spending less than you can actually afford. Don't purchase the highest-priced home that you can qualify for. Give yourself some margin. That is what living below your means is all about. Focus less on *looking* like you have money and focus more on actually *having* money.

Eliminate your debt. Practice living without debt. Develop a mindset of cash-based spending rather than credit-based spending. I know from experience that debt is easy to accumulate and can be very difficult to eliminate. In order to create prosperity, you must begin to live on what you have and eliminate the burden of needing to dedicate future financial resources to paying for things you probably could have done without in the first place. If you have debt, make debt elimination your number-one financial priority.

Save and invest. Make it your goal, if you are not already doing so, to save 20 percent of your net income. Invest it wisely and watch it grow. Save three to six months' living expenses as an emergency fund, and hold the money in a conservative account that you can access easily. Consider enlisting the services of a trustworthy advisor to help you develop a personal financial plan and an investment strategy.

Educate yourself about money. Particularly if you did not grow up learning about money or haven't been the greatest at handling money as an adult, spend some time reading and learning about how to create financial prosperity in your life. There are many great books and articles out there.

Give. Feeling powerful helps us develop and maintain a prosperity consciousness that attracts money to us. Few things make you feel more financially powerful than knowing that you have enough to give to others. No matter how little you have, God has blessed you with enough that you can give some of it to help others. Tithe where you worship. Give to a charity or worthy cause that you support. Share what you have with someone who you know is in need. Be willing to give of your financial resources, your skills, and your time to further good works.

Don't Let Age Block
Your Path to Success

The business world has changed quite a bit from when twenty-somethings rarely advanced to management positions and only rarely owned successful companies. Today, opportunities abound for twenty-somethings who are sharp, motivated and hard-working.

If you are a part of the under-thirty crowd, you've no doubt had to deal with the issue of your age. If you are fortunate, you work for a company that gives you the benefit of the doubt and allows you to prove yourself. Most companies fit into this category. If yours doesn't, it may be time to move on. It's important that you take the opportunity to prove yourself by making age a non-issue. Your age, in and of itself, is irrelevant. This is true whether you are young, old, or somewhere in between. What is relevant is how you contribute to your company's success.

Valorie Burton

While some twenty-somethings must deal with age bias on account of lack of work experience, others may encounter age bias for having *too much* work experience. In both instances, you can use similar principles to deal with the problem. Here are some ways you can make age a non-issue in your career.

Don't be embarrassed by your age. About a month after I was promoted to marketing director for Lane Gorman Trubitt, L.L.P., I attended a reception given for my company by a North Dallas law firm. One of the firm's partners was a graduate of my alma mater, Florida State University. When a partner from my company proudly introduced me, saying, "This is Valorie Burton, our marketing director. She went to Florida State, too," the attorney responded with interest. "Really? What year did you graduate?" Perhaps it was my paranoia, but it seemed everyone in the room was intent on hearing my answer. I was twenty-three and I barely looked it. I paused for a moment, then replied, "I graduated in '93." He stared at me with a blank look on his face—a look I expected. "Gee," he said, "I've never met anyone who graduated from FSU in the nineties before."

I felt slightly awkward, as though I was too young to be in the room. The truth of the matter was that I had no reason to feel awkward or embarrassed by my age.

Know your company. It's easy to focus so intently on the projects at hand that we forget that we are just one piece in a big puzzle. Take time out to learn the departments and divisions in your company. Understanding the big picture will help you better understand your job.

Don't be a know-it-all. The biggest disadvantage for a young businessperson is the lack of long years of experience. There is always something more to learn, and it is important to be willing to learn. Even if you think you know it all (and you don't), there's no need to act like it. It alienates you. For a more experienced businessperson, it is important to remain flexible. Don't allow your years of experience to make you "set in your ways." Be open to change and to trying new ways of doing things.

It's all in the attitude. Don't just do your job, do it exceptionally well. Make life easier for your boss. Use constructive criticism to your advantage by making needed improvements. It won't go unnoticed. Remember that your job is not your life, so don't waste energy holding grudges against people or going out of your way not to speak to someone. It's just not worth it.

Keep learning. Continuing education courses, seminars, books, and professional associations are excellent sources to

Valorie Burton

help you stay abreast of the trends in your industry and learn more effective ways to do your job. Be willing to continually learn and improve.

Be a solution; deliver results. In almost any profession, analytical and creative thinking are key components to success. When your company is seeking answers to a problem, don't be afraid to offer assistance. If you've done your homework and have an idea, suggest it. Even if the idea isn't used, you'll be perceived as a team player. When your ideas *are* accepted, be sure to deliver. The results will speak for themselves.

Live in the Moment

Live in the moment. Sounds simple enough, doesn't it? Then why does it seem that so many of us are continually focused on "what's next" without ever taking the time to enjoy "what's now"?

Wherever you are, practice *being* there—not just physically, but mentally. Have you ever talked to someone and gotten the distinct feeling that the person was acting as though they were listening to you yet their mind was somewhere else entirely? Perhaps it was their body language or expression that gave away their lack of interest in your conversation. We've all experienced the aggravation of talking to someone and not having their full attention. Or perhaps you have been the guilty party yourself?

When you talk to people, practice being with them right then at that moment. I practice this intently when I am with my brother, who is more than twenty years younger than I am. Recognizing that he won't be a kid for long, I savor the moments that we spend together. Whether I am taking him to the zoo, to a basketball game, or just playing with him, I try my best to be "in the moment."

Although it may not be the most pleasant thought, remember that tomorrow is not guaranteed. The one thing that you have for sure is the here and now. This is the space that you should strive to live in—not the past, because there is nothing that you can do to change it; and not the future, because it isn't here yet.

When you are constantly thinking about what's next, you never experience what's next when it comes. Why not? Because when "what's next" finally comes, you are already busy thinking about the next "what's next." Slow down! Stop moving so fast. Enjoy just being where you are, right now, in this moment.

Our "what's next" behavior manifests itself in many ways. In conversation, we can be so busy thinking about what we're going to say next that we don't listen to what the other person is saying. In our job, we can be so busy trying to get promoted that we don't take time to appreciate and enjoy our current position. Then when we get promoted, it's the same thing all over again. Where exactly does that "what's next" ladder finally end? In your personal life, do you take the time to enjoy the things that you have, or are you never satisfied, always wanting something bigger and better? A bigger house. A newer car. The latest gadget. It is great to want more out of life. In fact, it is a very good thing. But how about being happy with where you are in life at this moment and not totally consuming yourself with where you plan to be at some date in the future?

Try to live in the present. Whatever you are doing, give your full attention to it. It will take practice at first, but the more you live in the moment, the richer your life experiences will be.

———————

Cure Yourself of the Overdrive Syndrome

A problem that derives from over*load* is what I term the over*drive* syndrome. The overdrive syndrome is caused by living in a constant state of high stress. The eventual result is burnout. Imagine that you are driving your dream sports car down an open highway. You can drive as fast and as far as you want. You shift into overdrive and push the pedal as far as it will go. And then you just keep going at the maximum speed until the engine burns up or you run out of gas. Either way, the car stops. It won't go any farther until it is refilled and restored. That is the essence of the overdrive syndrome.

So often we move through life at warp speed. We shift into overdrive—operating on high stress and adrenaline—whether the situations we are in call for it or not. And when we come down, the fall can be pretty hard. Our bodies are exhausted. Our minds are still moving at a rapid pace. And we have taken little time to enjoy all that we have accomplished.

It is fine to shift into overdrive when necessary. The overdrive syndrome doesn't kick in until we decide to stay in overdrive indefinitely. We find ourselves in trouble when we set tight deadlines for *everything,* don't give ourselves time to get the important things in our lives done, and *never* slow down.

The first step to curing yourself of the overdrive syndrome is to recognize the problem. Here are few questions to ask yourself:

- Do you set deadlines for yourself that you are rarely able to meet?
- Do you rush everywhere you go?
- Do you regularly feel as though you are behind and rushing to catch up?
- Do you feel that you are rushing to be "first" or "ahead of the game" in your career, family, or finances?
- Do you get speeding tickets more than once a year?
- Do you operate best under an adrenaline rush?
- Are you uncomfortable doing nothing?
- When you take a break or a vacation, do you miss being "busy"?

- Do you feel as though you are constantly in a race to an invisible finish line?
- Do you prefer life in the fast lane—whether in your career or personal life?

If you answered yes to two or more of these questions, you may have a touch of the overdrive syndrome. The more questions you answered yes to, the more likely it is that you need to work toward curing yourself. Consider these prescriptions to remedy the problem:

- Be realistic about the deadlines you set for yourself. Give yourself the time you need to properly meet your goals, and give yourself a margin for error.
- Be conscious of your habit of rushing everywhere you go. Moving with a sense of urgency typically gives you the perception that you are getting ahead, but usually the reality is that you are simply causing yourself to be stressed, while arriving at the destination no sooner than anyone else.
- Life is not a race. Focus your energy inward and set goals for yourself without comparing yourself to others.
- Practice driving with patience.
- Walk with grace and ease.

- Commit yourself to completing projects and arriving for appointments ahead of schedule. Chronic procrastinators can begin by first setting aside time to catch up. Then make a realistic plan for completing future activities on time.
- Practice the art of doing nothing.

Valorie Burton

Understand That
Education = Preparation

Once you decide on a goal, it's time to roll up your sleeves and prepare to achieve it. What good is an opportunity if we aren't prepared to take advantage of it when it comes along? A tremendous part of preparation is education. No matter what the goal, if you are serious about achieving it, there is a relevant educational process. You may already have obtained the education that is needed by virtue of your experiences.

Education can be formal or informal. It depends entirely on the goal. If you are not sure of what you should do to prepare, do some informal research. Seek out others who have already achieved what you are aspiring to do, and find out what they did to prepare. This is an important step. Sometimes we think that we know what needs to be done to achieve a goal and we proceed accordingly. If, however, we ask someone who has already "been there," we might find out that our way will involve more time, energy, money, and trouble.

At a conference recently I sat in on a panel discussion about entrepreneurial ideas for communications professionals. An audience member who had a sincere interest in starting a public relations firm said that she was planning to go to graduate school first to get an MBA. This, she felt, would prepare her for running her own company. She asked members of the panel, all of whom were entrepreneurs, what they thought of her plan. Every single one of them (plus a few entrepreneurs who were sitting in the audience) advised against the idea. The fact is that you don't need an MBA to be an entrepreneur. There are issues that you will deal with when starting and growing a business that you will never learn, let alone master, from a grad-school textbook. Through hands-on experience and research you learn as much as possible about the type of business you want to start, and you can hire experts such as accountants, lawyers, and marketers to help you steer your business to success. The extensive resources that you would expend to earn an MBA could be spent building your business. Hopefully, the woman who posed that question to the panel is busy building a successful public relations firm rather than attending graduate school to "prepare" her for starting a business.

Valorie Burton

There are certainly many instances when an MBA, or some other type of formal education, is absolutely essential to the success formula for your goal. And if you already have the formal education, it can be like the icing on the cake when you are pursuing a goal. At other times, hands-on experience is the best way to go. Do research to find out what is the best method for your goal. Once you discover the answer, jump in wholeheartedly and learn everything you possibly can about the subject. With the right education, success is just around the corner.

Love Yourself First

If you hope to truly love others and live a fulfilling life, it is imperative that you first love yourself. Are you willing to bestow more love and respect on friends, a significant other, or family members than you do on yourself? Do you believe that by doing so you are able to get the love that you need? The truth is that all of the love you need is inside you. You must first unlock the power of your own self-love. Doing so enables you to engage in relationships from the healthy perspective of someone who already has the love that she needs most—her own.

Without self-love, you enter relationships as someone who is needy and dependent. You will constantly search and give anything for the love of others, but their love will never be enough. The neediness becomes a drain on your relationships. It is also likely, if you are in this situation, that you attract people into your life who complement your own dependency and neediness. They feel better as a result of their own ability to "save" you.

Once you discover your own true self-love, you are then able to give love unconditionally to the significant people in your life. You will also commit to doing things in your life that demonstrate your love for yourself. You will come to understand that you deserve the best, and as a result, you will live your life accordingly.

––––––––––––

Practice Patience

In today's fast-paced, stress-filled world, it seems that people are more frustrated and annoyed than ever at the slightest problems. Every business is racing to provide customers with super-speedy service and longer hours of operation. You can have your film developed in less than an hour. You can get your oil changed in ten minutes. Banks even promise to approve loans over the phone in five minutes. We have become so accustomed to this rushed service that we would be surprised if a company didn't offer this convenience. And what about twenty-four-hour service? From grocery stores to ATM machines to fast-food restaurants, the world is increasingly accommodating to people's desires to get what they want when they want it, and as quickly as possible. None of it, of course, encourages a spirit of patience in our everyday living. Instead, it seems that we have become more impatient than ever, resulting in frustration, stress, and

Valorie Burton

unnecessary annoyance. I am amazed at how easily people can be bothered, even over little things that in the grand scheme of life really don't matter much.

You can reverse this trend and allow patience to permeate your being by practicing it. Often, impatience results from behavior that treats every situation with urgency, even when it isn't warranted. We behave as though everything that we want we must have right this minute.

The vast majority of the time, we are operating on a false sense of urgency. Do you go through your everyday life as if everything that you do must be done in the shortest amount of time possible or you will be terribly inconvenienced? Whether you are standing in line at the grocery store or driving home in traffic, become aware of your false sense of urgency. When you feel it arise, take a deep breath and use the moment to practice patience.

Relax. Resolve not to drive home as though you are in the Daytona 500, repeatedly changing lanes to try to get ahead of the next person. Make a decision that you will be patient and that you will not approach your daily activities with a false sense of urgency.

If you tend to demonstrate a lack of patience in the routine activities of your everyday life, it is likely that the same attitude is also reflected in situations that are significant to you.

When it comes to dealing with family members, are you impatient? Does your household operate on a false sense of urgency as its normal mode of operation? When it comes to your career, do you easily become restless? Are you quick to change jobs? Are you unwilling to spend the time and energy necessary to excel at a level that would be worthy of a raise or promotion? Put in an honest and hard day's work. Relax. Be patient. Good things *do* come to those who wait.

Do Nice Things
(But Keep Them to Yourself!)

The older I get the more I admire my mother for being an absolutely beautiful person. Although she is outwardly attractive, her true beauty comes from within. She has a sweet and giving spirit that people sense, even upon meeting her for the first time. One of the most important lessons that she taught me is that you should willingly give to those in need. When you do so, she taught me, you should do it out of the desire of your heart and not because others are going to praise you for it. She didn't just tell me this. She practiced what she preached.

One winter when I was in high school, she noticed the extremely worn and raggedy shoes of an elderly man in our church. He had very obvious difficulty walking. He always wore the same shoes and the soles were nearly torn off. Upon talking to the man, who was always smiling and friendly, she learned that during Denver's horrible Blizzard of '82 he had been homeless. With no warm home to call his own, he endured bitter cold temperatures for far too long before finding warm shelter. His feet were severely frostbitten. As a result, there was extensive and permanent damage to both of his feet and one foot had to be partially amputated. My mother asked this stranger his shoe size and what kind of shoes he needed. Then she set out to find the kind of shoes he needed. She bought him two pairs of special shoes for Christmas that year. The man was so grateful and appreciative. She was equally as thankful for the opportunity to help someone who needed it.

During my sophomore year of college, I lived with my mom in Monterey, California, one of the most beautiful places in the country. Unfortunately, all of that beauty makes Monterey one of the most expensive places in which to live. Like many cities, it has its share of homeless people. My mother had noticed one of these homeless people, a man who regularly camped out on the side of a 7-Eleven store that she frequented. On Sundays, when she cooked dinner, she fixed a plate for this man. I am sure that he must have thought she was nothing short of an angel. She would wrap a complete homemade dinner, with all of the fixings—including a big slice of lemon meringue pie—in plastic and put it in a bag with plastic silverware and a can of pop. Then she would

Valorie Burton

drive down to the 7-Eleven and give it to him. Sometimes, she even put a book in the bag after she noticed that he often sat on the sidewalk and read. She did this once a week without telling anyone about her good deeds. She did it out of compassion, purely for the sake of helping someone in need. After I moved to California, I went with her one Sunday to deliver the meal. This older, homeless man was so glad to see my mother drive up. I handed the dinner to him, he thanked me, and I headed back to the car. Just as I closed the door, I looked up and the man was running toward the car with a withered red rose, his token of appreciation. That small gesture so warmed my heart that I understood at that very moment why it is better to give than to receive.

I believe that all of us have the opportunity to be used by God as an angel to help someone in need without any expectation of recognition for our deeds.

Volunteer

I have found few things more rewarding than the feeling I get from helping others or making someone's day brighter. As a middle school student, I remember the friendships I made with elderly people as part of the Adopt-a-Grandparent program that was sponsored by my school. By the time I was eleven years old, I had lost three of my own four grandparents. My maternal grandfather died before I was born. However, I spent eight of my summers, between the ages of three and eleven, with my father's parents in Anderson, South Carolina. Those summers were magical, and they gave me the opportunity to spend precious time with relatives on both sides of my family since my parents grew up in the same hometown. My grandparents' deaths when I was nine and eleven were devastating to me. For a couple of months every summer, Grandmama and Granddaddy had been like a second set of parents in my life. Volunteering in the Adopt-a-

Grandparent program gave me the chance to connect with people who were my grandparents' age. I really enjoyed that.

Likewise, you can choose a charity that means a great deal to you for personal reasons or simply because you believe in the cause. Volunteering gives you the gratification of knowing that you are making a difference in the community. What are your special gifts? What could you do to help a local charity?

Perhaps you would like to help out on an administrative level, by serving on a board or committee, or helping with fundraising or public relations. Although this type of volunteerism isn't direct service to those being served by the organization, it is very valuable work. For four years, I served on the board of directors of Girls Incorporated of Metropolitan Dallas (formerly known as Girls Club), a fabulous non-profit organization that serves girls from areas of the city with higher poverty, teenage-pregnancy, and high school dropout rates. The program is extremely successful at helping girls beat the odds in their community and live successful, responsible lives. Interacting with these smart, confident girls helps me remember that my active involvement on the board makes a positive difference in my community.

I grew up seeing my dad volunteer in the Big Brothers program in Denver. His "little brother" was about nine years old when my dad started mentoring him. For my dad, the experience of being a role model for this smart, athletically gifted little boy was great. For his little brother, who was biracial, having a positive male role model—particularly an African-American—was important, since his Italian-American mother was the only parent in his household. Soon my dad was volunteering as the coach of his little league football and baseball teams. We made it a family affair, and my mother and I often attended the games to cheer both of them on.

Volunteering doesn't always require an ongoing commitment. One of my most memorable Thanksgiving holidays was in 1991, when I was living in Monterey. I went with my stepfather's eighty-year-old Aunt Alberta to a soup kitchen to help serve food to people who couldn't afford a Thanksgiving feast like the ones that millions of us enjoy every year. What a wonderful way to show thanks—by giving back to those who are less fortunate than you. That type of volunteer activity requires only a one-time commitment of a couple of hours. We can all spare two hours once a year, can't we? Hopefully, you can spare even more.

Understand Rather than Judge

Have you ever encountered someone you didn't like but with whom you had to deal on a regular basis regardless?

Maybe it is someone you work with, a neighbor, a classmate, or even a relative. Dealing with difficult people doesn't always have to be hard. Remember that everything you do is a choice, including how you choose to deal with people you sometimes wish you didn't have to.

In his book *The 7 Habits of Highly Effective People* author Stephen R. Covey says seek first to understand, then to be understood. I have found that when I truly seek to understand other people, I am not nearly as frustrated, annoyed, or upset by the things they do. I recognize that their behavior is a symptom of issues in their life that they have yet to deal with. You may think that someone at your job hates you for no good reason at all, that the person's behavior toward you is petty and jealous. If you dig a little deeper, however, and try to get an understanding of the person's behavior, you may just learn that they don't hate you at all. Instead, what they see in you may be what they want for themselves but haven't taken the initiative to get. They don't hate you. They hate themselves, and their self-hatred is reflected in their behavior toward you.

When you come to understand this, your attitude toward them changes for the better. Instead of reacting to the person's behavior, which is a symptom of a deeper issue, you now seek to understand the root cause of that behavior—the deeper issue. Just knowing that there is a deeper issue is often enough to give us the compassion and patience that we need to deal with such people without our blood pressure skyrocketing every time we encounter them. For many difficult people, satisfaction comes from getting a "rise" out of you. Their power stems from an ability to control other people's behavior. The more bothered you are, the more motivated they are to keep bothering you. Observe the interaction between someone you consider to be difficult and several other people. Does he or she seem to be difficult with some people and not others? People take their cues about how to treat you . . . from *you*. If you return nasty behavior with calm behavior, you can diffuse a potentially difficult situation.

Valorie Burton

How you deal with difficult people is a choice. First, choose to understand the other person. Second, don't add fuel to the fire when someone is trying to get a rise out of you. And, lastly, depending on the situation, choose to spend less time in the presence of difficult people.

———————

Forgive and Let Go of Grudges

Few things steal your time and energy like holding a grudge. If a person has wronged you in some way, why allow him or her to continue to disrupt your life by invading your thoughts? Sometimes we let things that have happened to us in the past overpower our present. We hold on to them because they hurt us so much and we can't make sense of them. We can't understand the person's actions or thoughts. As a result, we don't want to forgive him or her. Or perhaps we want to forgive, but we search our hearts and can't seem to find it there to truly forgive.

Not only is forgiveness essential to our own peace of mind, but God requires that in order for *us* to be forgiven, we must forgive *others*. If we do not forgive others, then none of our transgressions (and we all have them) are forgiven. Often people do not forgive others because they do not believe that they are forgiven for the things that they have done wrong.

Valorie Burton

Their hearts are hardened to the idea of forgiveness. Others have not been merciful and granted them forgiveness, so why, they ask themselves, should they forgive others? It is impossible to understand the miracle of forgiveness when you do not believe that you are forgiven for the mistakes that you have made. It is similar to the principle of trust. There are those who are untrusting of others because they have been betrayed in the past. And then there are those who are untrusting of others because they are untrustworthy themselves. Likewise, if you are unforgiving, it is quite likely that you believe that you have not been forgiven. So what should you do?

You should pray about it. Pray that you will feel compassion for yourself and others. Pray for understanding. Pray for the ability to let go of the past. And, most importantly, pray for the desire and strength to forgive.

Interestingly, people often *say* that they have forgiven while still holding grudges against those whom they supposedly forgave. They remain angry and bitter toward the person. A spirit of forgiveness does not hold grudges. I have made it my policy not to hold grudges. It is a policy that truly tests my faith sometimes. I have encountered situations where people who I thought were my friends completely betrayed my trust, treated me badly, and never apologized for doing so. Such situations left me feeling sad, angry, disgusted, and foolish all at once. I would let the situation replay in my mind over and over again—each time, conjuring up images that led to more resentment against those involved. I had to learn to pray about it and let it go. Letting go of past hurt or betrayal is a process. We should not expect that we can change our feelings in an instant. Only the healing power of God can change our hearts and lead us to forgive without holding a grudge. This kind of Divine inspiration can even lead us to pray for those who would otherwise be classified as our enemies. One of the greatest signs of spiritual maturity is your ability to forgive.

Valorie Burton

Visit a New Place at Least Once a Year

It can be easy to settle into your surroundings and forget, even if only for a while, that your immediate surroundings are just a small piece of an infinitely bigger world. One of the best ways to make sure that you see more of the world is to make a promise to yourself to visit at least one new place every year. The experience of traveling can be fun, romantic, educational, adventurous, or whatever you choose it to be. Most important, it will broaden your horizons by opening your mind to people and places different from your own.

Growing up in an Air Force family, I learned quite a bit about different people and cultures. U.S. military bases are some of the most diverse places in American society. Not only are they made up of the diverse American population, but they also include spouses from foreign countries who met their military husbands or wives while those service-people were on assignment abroad. As a result, there are also many children of a variety of mixed-race backgrounds to be found on U.S. military bases. I am glad to have grown up around so much diversity. What I have always enjoyed most about traveling is the adventure of going somewhere I have never been before and meeting people who are different from everyone back home. It is nice to get a new perspective on life every once and a while.

You deserve the benefit of travel. Don't just talk about the places that you are going to travel to "someday." Start making plans for where you are going to travel this year. I am partial to traveling abroad at least once per year, but I also like to explore new places around the country and around my own state.

Make a list of ideal places that you would like to visit. Where do you want to go first? When do you want to go? What do you need to do to get ready? Now, make it happen.

Bon voyage!

Reward Yourself!

In our daily routines, we often move from one project to the next at warp speed. There can be so much going on in our lives that we forget to stop for a moment and savor our victories, big or small, before moving on to something else. Eventually, the non-stop string of activities and projects can lead to burnout. Take time out during your schedule to reward yourself for the progress you are making, or simply for a job well done. You may find that if you don't reward yourself, no one else will.

In your everyday life, give yourself small rewards during the workday, such as a break and a stretch every hour, or after you have completed a specific task. This can work as an incentive, particularly when you are working on a task that is not all that much fun. Having something to look forward to can motivate you to stay focused on the task at hand and, ultimately, finish more quickly. For bigger projects or activities, think of bigger ways to reward yourself. Perhaps you should take a day off, get a massage, spring for a pair of tickets to see your favorite sports team or a play that you've heard good things about. Maybe you should reward yourself with a vacation. Whatever the accomplishment, reward yourself accordingly. The self-motivational benefits will pay off. Self-rewarding can also be an effective motivational tool if you are working with a group, particularly if you are managing the group. Set up milestones for the entire group. In order to be rewarded, everyone in the group must successfully complete his or her piece of the project. Everyone, including you, is rewarded for the success of the group. This type of approach to motivation fosters commitment, teamwork, and a sense of gratification when the goal is reached. Group rewards can be effective, whether you are managing a department in a company, teaching students in a classroom, coaching an athletic team, or raising a family.

Take a moment to give some thought to the kinds of rewards that you would like to receive from yourself for a job well done. List them here.

Small rewards during your daily routine:

_____

_____

Valorie Burton

_____

_____

Rewards for significant accomplishments:

_____

_____

_____

_____

Rewards for accomplishing a major goal:

_____

_____

_____

_____

Pamper-ize Yourself

So many of us think of pampering as a luxury to be enjoyed only *occasionally*. But pampering should be a regular part of your life. A guaranteed way to enrich your life is to *prioritize* pampering in your life. I call it "pamper-izing." Making pampering a priority is one of the best ways to decrease your stress level and increase your sense of inner peace.

In her book *Sacred Pampering Principles,* author Debrena Jackson Gandy calls pampering "inner grooming," so as not to confuse pampering with "outer grooming" activities such as manicures and trips to the hair salon. According to my friend Paula McClure, a longtime television personality who owns the Paula McClure Mood Spa in Dallas, pampering is about bringing nurturing and relaxation to your mind, body, and spirit.

Pampering is about discovering and enjoying your own personal calming rituals. Through these rituals, a personal transformation can take place. You begin to connect with yourself on a deeper level as you give yourself the attention you so richly deserve. As pampering becomes a part of your normal routine, you will begin to reap some wonderful benefits. Some of the benefits of pampering include:

- stress reduction
- enhanced confidence level
- clearer insight on your goals
- improved complexion
- a calmer and more relaxed outlook on life
- a more positive attitude

With so many potential benefits, why do so many people neglect to pamper themselves? The typical answers usually begin with "I don't have the time . . ." or "I don't have the money. . . ." Pampering yourself doesn't have to be a luxury that you must do without because of a lack of time or money. Over the years, pampering has earned a reputation as something that is only for wealthy women with loads of time on their hands. No doubt about it, if you've got time and money, there are some wonderful ways that you can find to treat yourself to plenty of luxurious pampering. But there are also numerous inexpensive ways to pamper yourself in the comfort of your own home. Schedule time once or twice a week for pampering. You can begin by filling your home with relaxing scents. At any number of stores in the mall you will find aromatherapy candles and potpourri to enrich your favorite room or your whole home. Your bathtub is the best pampering tool in your house. Why not put it to frequent use? Most of us choose hasty showers over baths, whether we are in a hurry or not.

Set aside a couple of times a week for a warm, relaxing bubble bath with your favorite aromatherapy bath crystals. Dim the lights or turn them off completely and light the bathroom with candles. Lie there in the tub and relax. Give yourself a facial once a week during your pampering time. Reward yourself and go to a spa for a massage, facial, and/or pedicure. If you are looking for a cost-effective massage, consider taking a couples massage class at your local continuing-education center or make a massage appointment at a reputable massage school. Take turns with your spouse or significant other giving each other massages. Make pampering a priority in your life by scheduling time for it, just as you do all of your other activities. Let others in the house know not to disturb you during this time. Turn off the phone. Enjoy!

Valorie Burton

Make Your Home Your Sanctuary

The one place where you should feel comfortable, relaxed, and even pampered, is in your own home. Whether you live in a 10,000-square-foot mansion or a 500-square-foot apartment, your home should take on a personality that is a reflection of you. It should be a sanctuary from the stress and chaos of the rest of the world. It should be a place that you look forward to retreating to because you simply enjoy being there. In my condo, I have created an environment of sights, sounds, and scents that help me relax and unwind at the end of a hectic day. This also helps stimulate creativity when I write.

In fact, as I write these words, I am curled up in my favorite chair in my lavender-painted bedroom, inhaling the sweet aroma of a candle that is burning on my dresser, enjoying the Saturday-morning sunlight as it beams through my window, and listening to one of my favorite jazz CDs by

South African guitarist Jonathan Butler. I am in a state of peace and relaxation. I have temporarily disconnected myself from the outside world so that I can concentrate my thoughts and energy inward—no television blaring, and the telephone ringer is turned off. I am in the peaceful environment of my own space.

Too often, it seems, people do not give much thought to the environment that they haphazardly create in their own home. Family members watch television more than they talk to each another. The people in the household shout down the hall or up the stairs rather than walk a few feet to ask a question in a normal tone of voice. And, worst of all, there is clutter everywhere! Now, it certainly is understandable that some people are neat freaks while others are just prone to be junky. However, it is important to understand that the removal of clutter can actually have psychological benefits. Clutter is a visible sign of stress and chaos. Take note of the accumulation of clutter in spaces where you spend a great deal of your time, such as your car, your home, or your office. I can usually tell when my life is overloaded by how much clutter has invaded my space. It usually doesn't happen overnight, but over the course of a few days or weeks, until I just can't take it anymore! Once I remove the clutter, though, my mind is clearer and I don't feel as overwhelmed.

Valorie Burton

Because your home is the place where you rest, recharge, and start each day, make sure that it is as clutter-free and inviting for you as possible. Decorate it in a style that suits you. Keep pictures of family, friends, and important places visible so that you are reminded every day of the people who are blessings in your life. Paint your walls a color that you like and that will enhance your mood. Sometimes, even the smallest changes can make a big difference in your home environment. Start right now by thinking of just one thing that would enhance your home—and then do it.

————————

Learn to Network

Business for The Burton Agency is based almost entirely on referrals. Clients and associates refer business to the agency when they know of a potential client who is in need of marketing or public relations services. They say, "You should call The Burton Agency." And the rest is up to us. Everyone at The Burton Agency is involved in the community and networks regularly. One of the best things that you can do for your career is to meet as many people as possible. Develop reciprocal relationships in which you are just as willing to help others as they are to help you. By doing so, you will always have options—whether you are looking to make a job change, bring in a new client, or just need career advice.

Networking provides a competitive advantage in just about every line of business. It is not only a crucial means of gaining new business, but also a great way to stay abreast of industry trends, develop friendships, and maintain employment options. Networking can be an intimidating exercise for those who don't enjoy mingling with people they don't know. The first time I attended a business function and had to mix with strangers, I felt completely awkward. A hundred questions ran through my mind. Who should I talk to? What should I say? How do I stand here and not look like an idiot? It would certainly be useful if colleges would teach Networking 101. But since they don't, consider the following advice a postgraduate short course.

Before the Event

Obviously, some events will be much easier than others. When you attend luncheons or other functions of the professional associations to which you belong, striking up a conversation with a complete stranger can be quite easy. Since everyone works in a similar career field, you naturally will have things in common.

If the event is not specific to your industry, finding a topic of conversation doesn't have to lead to an awkward exchange of half-sentences and silent pauses. Before the function, think of a few things to talk about so that conversation won't lag. Think about what you may have in common with the people that you will meet. If you expect a considerable age gap between you and most of the other people at the function, don't let that bother you. It's not an issue unless you make it one.

At the Event

Bring someone with you if you are uncomfortable with the idea of striking up conversation with people you don't know. Having someone to talk to between conversations can make you feel less self-conscious. However, I challenge you to attend some functions alone. It is a great exercise in self-confidence to know that you can go places alone. It is a way to meet people that you might not otherwise meet if you are with someone else.

If your intent is to meet as many people as possible, show up early. Smile and be friendly. It will draw people to you. Remember that first impressions are lasting ones.

Since it's rude to talk and eat at the same time, it is a good idea to come early, eat first, and then mingle. Besides, how can you shake someone's hand with a plate in one hand and a drink in the other?

Look for the person who isn't talking to anyone and would welcome your conversation. When you introduce yourself, read the person's name tag (if they're wearing one) and use their name. If the company is on the name tag as well, it can be an easy segue into conversation. Give a brief intro-

Valorie Burton

duction of yourself and what you do—something that is interesting and to the point. Be sure to ask them about themselves and listen to their answers before going into detail about yourself. People are always willing to talk about themselves. If you show an interest in them, they will want to know more about you.

If your intent is to meet a lot of people, don't spend too much time with one person. Move on and meet other people. Be sure to get a business card and write notes on the back when you leave so that you will remember the person later.

After the Event

Depending on your goal, be sure to follow up with the contacts that you've made. Short notes or follow-up calls can make a lasting impression and often open the door to lasting business relationships and friendships.

Write Handwritten Letters
and Make an Impact

In this age of e-mail and five-cents-per-minute long-distance phone calls, it seems that handwritten letters are an endangered species. By the same token, because letters are so rare, receiving one seems to have more meaning than ever before. Taking the time to sit down and write a letter allows you to slow down for a moment and show your appreciation to someone in a very personal way. You can always pick up the phone and call someone to say thanks for something they did, or simply to let them know that you are thinking about them. You should. And it can be even faster to type a quick e-mail expressing the same sentiments. I am not discouraging that either. But there is something valuable that you give to someone when you sit down, write a letter by hand, and mail it—your time and energy. Your letter doesn't have to be long to make an impact. It needs to be heartfelt,

Valorie Burton

even if it's only three sentences. It is quite possible that on the day that the person opens the letter, yours will be the only handwritten item in their mailbox. Everything else might be bills, other business correspondence, and junk mail. Amidst all of that, your note will be quite appreciated. Another bonus to letters is that they have a sense of permanence. If what you say in the letter is particularly special or heartwarming, it is likely that the person on the receiving end will keep it.

I have kept several special letters that I received because of things that I do through The Burton Agency. I received a letter in August of 1997 from Ebby Halliday Acers, who had just been honored with the Texas Trailblazer Award. I created that award as a community-relations initiative for Lane Gorman Trubitt, L.L.P., while I was their marketing director. Today, it is an independent charitable luncheon that I continue to chair. It honors women who have achieved significant leadership roles in business and/or the community. I chair the event each year and as a result had gotten to know Ms. Halliday during the weeks leading up to the award luncheon. An incredible woman in her late eighties, she goes to work every day at the company she founded in 1945. Ebby Halliday Realtors is the largest privately held, residential real estate company in the nation. You can imagine my delight at receiving a sweet letter from her that said, among other things, "I hope our paths cross again, Valorie. I have great admiration for you." It is one of the few letters that I have framed and have hanging on my office wall. Over the years, I have received several letters from her. They are always thoughtful and always make me smile. When you write letters, aim to do the same. If you don't have much to say, that's fine. Something like this is great:

Dear Kim,

> *I thought of you today and wanted simply to say thanks for being a great friend. Your friendship is a blessing. Take care. I hope all is well.*

Love, Valorie

I didn't used to be much of a note- and letter-writer, but it's something I decided I *should* be. To get myself in the habit of writing, I went to a card store and bought matching stationary and envelopes. I also keep a supply of blank note cards, birthday cards, and thank-you cards in my office, so that when I feel inspired to write someone, I have everything that I need on hand. Why not start writing today? Think of one person you would like to write—a family member, old friend, teacher, former co-worker, or someone you don't know but sincerely admire. You will never run out of people to write to. Before you start reading the next mini-chapter, go ahead and write a letter. Ten minutes from now, you will be finished and in a few days, someone will have a smile on their face when they open the mailbox and see a piece of mail from you!

––––––––––

Spend Time with Yourself

Growing up as an only child, I got plenty of practice at spending time with myself. I think it made me a more analytical and self-reflective person. I am comfortable doing things and going places alone. And in that regard I'm lucky, because we all need to schedule some time when we are in the presence of only ourselves. It is during this time that you are able to escape the noise, problems, and opinions of everyone else and completely focus on you. If you rarely have the opportunity to be alone because you are taking care of children or loved ones, make an appointment with yourself after everyone goes to bed, or early in the morning before everyone wakes up. Use the time to do whatever you want to do—read a book, relax, scan the newspaper, do a crossword puzzle, or write in your journal. The idea is simply to spend quality time with yourself on a regular basis.

If you have a flexible schedule, there are a host of other

Valorie Burton

activities you can do with yourself. Take a walk, ride your bicycle, go to the park and read under a tree, take yourself out to breakfast, lunch, or dinner, or go to the movies. I have found that spending time with myself keeps me centered and focused. By being attentive to myself, I also am better able to be attentive to those around me.

I have known people who were leading disoriented, dysfunctional lives. Their biggest problem was that they were starving for their own attention. They were so caught up in meeting the needs of everyone around them that they never managed to meet their own needs. You have to put you first. This is not to suggest that you should be selfish or self-centered in a negative way. What I am suggesting is that when you take time for yourself, you have more energy to give of yourself to others. Your own attention is food for your soul. Make sure that you are being fed well and often.

Stress: Less, Not More

We are bombarded with books, news stories, and advice about how we can do more. Today people are doing more, seeing more, absorbing more, and handling more than at any other time in history. Life moves at a much faster pace than it used to. Technological advancements are great, but don't allow the fruits of modern-day technology to overrun your life. In today's world, many people are so connected that they have hardly a free moment during their waking hours. Digital phones, pagers, e-mail, laptops, car modems, home offices, home fax machines, and voice mail are incredible conveniences. But if these things keep you constantly "wired," the stress level can begin to spin out of control.

We survived for thousands of years without digital phones, pagers, e-mail, laptops, car modems, fax machines, and voice mail. In fact, just twenty years ago, most of us had never heard of any of these modern-day "necessities." When

Valorie Burton

people wanted to reach you, they had to call you, either at home or at work. If no one was there to answer the phone, they called back later. Getting in touch with you while you were grocery shopping was not an option.

Of course, technological niceties are just one facilitator of stress. A recent study shows that Americans work more hours than workers in any other industrialized nation. In the 1990s, we even surpassed Japan in the average number of hours worked annually per person. We also weigh more than we used to. This isn't exactly a healthy combination.

My suggestion? Lower your stress tolerance level. Take on fewer activities, not more. Give more thought to which activities are most important to you. Designate a time of the day when your house is disconnected from the world. This is your stress-reduction period. Don't answer the phone. Voice mail or the answering machine will get it—or you can check your caller ID later, right? Turn off the television and the radio. If you want to play music, put on a CD or tape. Don't log onto the Internet during your stress-reduction period. Your e-mail messages aren't going anywhere. Use this time to reconnect with yourself and your family or others in the household.

As you carry out your everyday activities, think less stress, not more. It seems that we are taught to admire people who can handle heaps of stress. It is as if being stressed somehow makes you appear more important because you have so much to do. To the contrary, the most successful people I have met are not overstressed. They lead balanced lives. They understand that too much stress is counterproductive and robs you of the joy of your everyday activities. Do you find that instead of enjoying the things you used to love, you now dread them? If you are stressed out, you may even begin to resent being asked for help because you view everything as an infringement on your time—time that you don't have.

As you strive to achieve success in your life, learn to work smarter, not harder. And think less stress, not more.

Valorie Burton

Create Your Own Opportunities

As someone who believes in making things happen even when the prospect of success looks grim to others, I get a bit annoyed when people say that they can't accomplish something that they really want to do. More often than not, you can find an alternative way to make something happen. You may determine that the alternative way is not worth your effort, but let *that* be your reason for not reaching the goal rather than simply concluding that it cannot be done.

There is an abundance of opportunity around you every day. Are you willing to make something of it? Are you willing to create it? A rich mind creates an opportunity that may seem impossible to others. Everything you need to succeed is already within you. You must be willing to make the effort and spend the time necessary to make your success happen.

Never forget that with God, all things are possible. Rely on Him as you pursue your goals, and as the old gospel hymn says, "He will make a way out of no way." When I decided to write this book, I created the opportunity for myself. Rather than quit when faced with the difficulty of finding a publisher, I decided to follow in the footsteps of numerous authors who have self-published and gone on to tremendous success. I created my own publishing company, named it Pearl Books after my dearly missed grandmother "Mama Pearl," and put my marketing and public relations background to good use. The process was exciting and the sense of accomplishment awesome.

It is incredible to see how an opportunity we create can lead to bigger opportunities. That's exactly what happened with this book. Seven months after I self-published *Rich Minds, Rich Rewards,* it was picked up by a major publishing house. The journey on which this book has led me has been truly rewarding.

Equally rewarding is the knowledge that this book can help you better your life. Remember my mission, which I shared earlier? "To create and enjoy a fulfilling, prosperous, and charitable life, and to inspire others to do the same." By making *Rich Minds, Rich Rewards* a reality, I am contributing to my life's mission. It is a wonderful feeling indeed.

What opportunity can you create that will help you further your mission in life? I hope that you will soon discover

Valorie Burton

your answer and pursue it with passion. My sincere wish is that these fifty-two mini-chapters have helped you enhance, empower, and enrich your everyday life. And remember— don't think that just because you've finished reading the book you can't come back and revisit these pages when you need to!

Wishing you the very richest rewards,

Valorie

Planning a Discussion

The issues in *Rich Minds, Rich Rewards* lend themselves to exciting conversation. The following are topics and questions that you can use to facilitate a discussion for book clubs, discussion groups, social gatherings, or parties.

For your book club or discussion group, it is helpful to choose a moderator who can read excerpts from the book aloud to the group and then ask questions for discussion. Or you may simply want to have a casual discussion among friends. The idea is to exchange ideas and opinions and, hopefully, to encourage one another.

Discussion Topic 1: Personal Fulfillment and Money

See the mini-chapters "Do What You Love and the Rewards Will Come," "Don't Downsize Your Dream," and "Change Your Ways to Change Your Life."

Does society teach us that work should be hard and that what we love should be just a hobby? Or do we learn that in our families? Can you really make money doing what you love? Why do people often settle for doing work that they don't love? Are you doing what you love for a living right now? What keeps you from pursuing what you love?

Discussion Topic 2: Life Purpose

See the mini-chapters "Have a Mission" and "Create Your Mission Statement."

How do you know when you have discovered your mission or life purpose? Did you stumble upon your mission or have you always known what it was? Are you still trying to discover your mission? What is your mission? How are you fulfilling it?

Discussion Topic 3: Communicating with Others

See the mini-chapters "Personal PR" and "Write Handwritten letters and Make an Impact."

Is letter-writing a lost art? Is it better to receive a handwritten note or an e-mail? Does it matter? Has technology taken the personal touch out of communication? If so, how?

Discussion Topic 4: Forgiveness

See the mini-chapter "Forgive and Let Go of Grudges."

Is it more stressful to hold a grudge or to let it go? Should we forgive in every situation? Should we not only forgive, but forget too? How do you know when someone is holding a grudge against another person even though they say they have forgiven the person?

Discussion Topic 5: Money

See the mini-chapter "Take Control of Your Financial Life."

Why are so many Americans in debt? Should money management be a required course for high school and college students? Where did you learn your money-management skills? What could you do to increase your income in the near future?

Discussion Topic 6: Decreasing Your Stress Level

See the mini-chapters "Cure Yourself of the Overdrive Syndrome," "Meditate," "Allow Peace to Guide Your Decisions," and "Stress: Less, Not More."

Does society pressure us to be busy all of the time? Why do Americans seem to always be in a hurry? Have the technological conveniences that are meant to save time (such as pagers, mobile phones, and e-mail) made people more overloaded? Does a healthy spiritual life help a person create a less stressful lifestyle?

Discussion Topic 7: Being Good to Yourself

See mini-chapters "Pamper-ize Yourself," "Reward Yourself!," "Spend Time with Yourself," "Love Yourself First," and "Visit a New Place at Least Once a Year."

What keeps people from pampering themselves on a regular basis? How do you like to pamper yourself? Do you find solutions to problems more easily when you are able to spend time alone? What new place would you like to visit and why?

Discussion Topic 8: Creating an Inspired Environment

See mini-chapter "Make Your Home Your Sanctuary."

Planning a Discussion

What makes a home warm and inviting? How does clearing clutter from your home affect your mood? How does the presence of clutter affect your mood? How can couples and families compromise to make their home a sanctuary for everyone who lives there?

Discussion Topic 9: Learning from Mistakes

See mini-chapters "Use Failure as a Learning Tool," "Don't Make Excuses," and "Don't Play the Blame Game."

Have you ever failed at something that led you to a better opportunity? Is failure God's way of moving you in a new direction? What is the best way to handle people who always blame others for their problems? Are there instances in which it is okay to make excuses?

Discussion Topic 10: Making a Difference

See mini-chapters "Do Nice Things (But Keep Them to Yourself!)" and "Volunteer."

Have people become more or less compassionate in recent years? How has volunteering or making a difference in another person's life impacted your life?

Suggested Reading

*The following are books that I have read,
enjoyed, and highly recommend.*

All the Joy You Can Stand, Debrena Jackson Gandy

Clear Your Clutter with Feng Shui, Karen Kingston

Don't Sweat the Small Stuff, Dr. Richard Carlson

In the Meantime, Iyanla Vanzant

In the Spirit, Susan Taylor

Lessons in Living, Susan Taylor

Life Makeovers, Cheryl Richardson

Maximize the Moment, Bishop T. D. Jakes

Sacred Pampering Principles, Debrena Jackson Gandy

The 7 Habits of Highly Effective People, Steven R. Covey

Take Time for Your Life, Cheryl Richardson

The Art of Doing Nothing, Veronique Vienne

The Artist's Way, Julia Cameron

The Black Woman's Guide to Financial Independence, Cheryl
   Broussard

The Courage to Be Rich, Suze Orman

The Lady, Her Lover and Her Lord, Bishop T. D. Jakes

The Millionaire Next Door, Thomas Stanley and William
Danko

The Millionaire's Path, Mark Fisher with Marc Allen

The Overload Syndrome, Dr. Richard Swenson

The Personal Touch, Terrie Williams

A Conversation with Author Valorie Burton

Q: Why did you write this book?

A: After I had the epiphany about my life purpose that I described in the introduction, I thought and prayed about what type of first book to write. I felt led to write an easy-to-read, inspiring guide to living a more fulfilling life that was geared toward people from all walks of life.

Q: What is your writing process?

A: When I write, I imagine that I am writing to a friend. It makes the process more relaxed, and, hopefully, the reader feels that I am writing directly to him or her. I wrote the entire book in longhand. I find that the words flow more easily for me when I write with pen and paper rather than at a computer. Also, I want to be used as a vessel to deliver messages of Divine inspiration. So each time I sat down to write the mini-chapters for *Rich Minds, Rich Rewards,* I prayed for wisdom and that I would write words touching readers in such a way that they would feel empowered to make positive changes in their lives.

Q: Who inspires you the most and why?

A: God inspires me most because the abundance of His grace and blessings never cease to amaze me. I am also inspired by everyday people who make their mark on the world by making a positive difference in the lives of others and by those who have the courage to live their dreams.

Q: What is next for you? Are you writing another book?
A: I am writing my second book now. It's called *Shifting out of Overdrive*. It is about slowing down, finding joy, and doing the things that matter most. I believe it will strike a chord with a lot of people.

Q: You are a Life Enrichment Specialist. What is that exactly?
A: Through my workshops, speaking engagements, website, articles, and books, I teach people simple yet powerful ways to enrich their lives. "Life Enrichment Specialist" seems the best way to describe what I do.

A Conversation with Author Valorie Burton

About the Author

VALORIE BURTON is a writer, professional speaker, and life-enrichment specialist. She speaks throughout the country, inspiring audiences to live more fulfilling, less stressful lives. Ms. Burton is also the founder and president of Burton-Metzger, a public relations firm in Dallas, Texas. She is a graduate of Florida State University, and at age twenty-one earned a master's degree in journalism from Florida A&M University. She is a former Miss Black Texas USA, Miss Black USA top-ten finalist, and a runner-up to Miss Texas. An Air Force "brat," she grew up in Florida, Germany, Colorado, and California, and now lives in Texas.

To receive the *Rich Minds, Rich Rewards* e-newsletter, e-mail Valorie, or learn more ways to enhance, enrich, and empower your life, visit Valorie Burton online at *www.valorieburton.com.*

To book Valorie for a speaking engagement, contact:

Valorie Burton Unlimited
P.O. Box 801344
Dallas, Texas 75380-1344
(214) 522-5544